ART STUDIO

GREAT PAINTINGS TO COLOUR IN

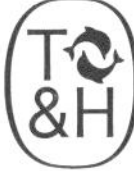

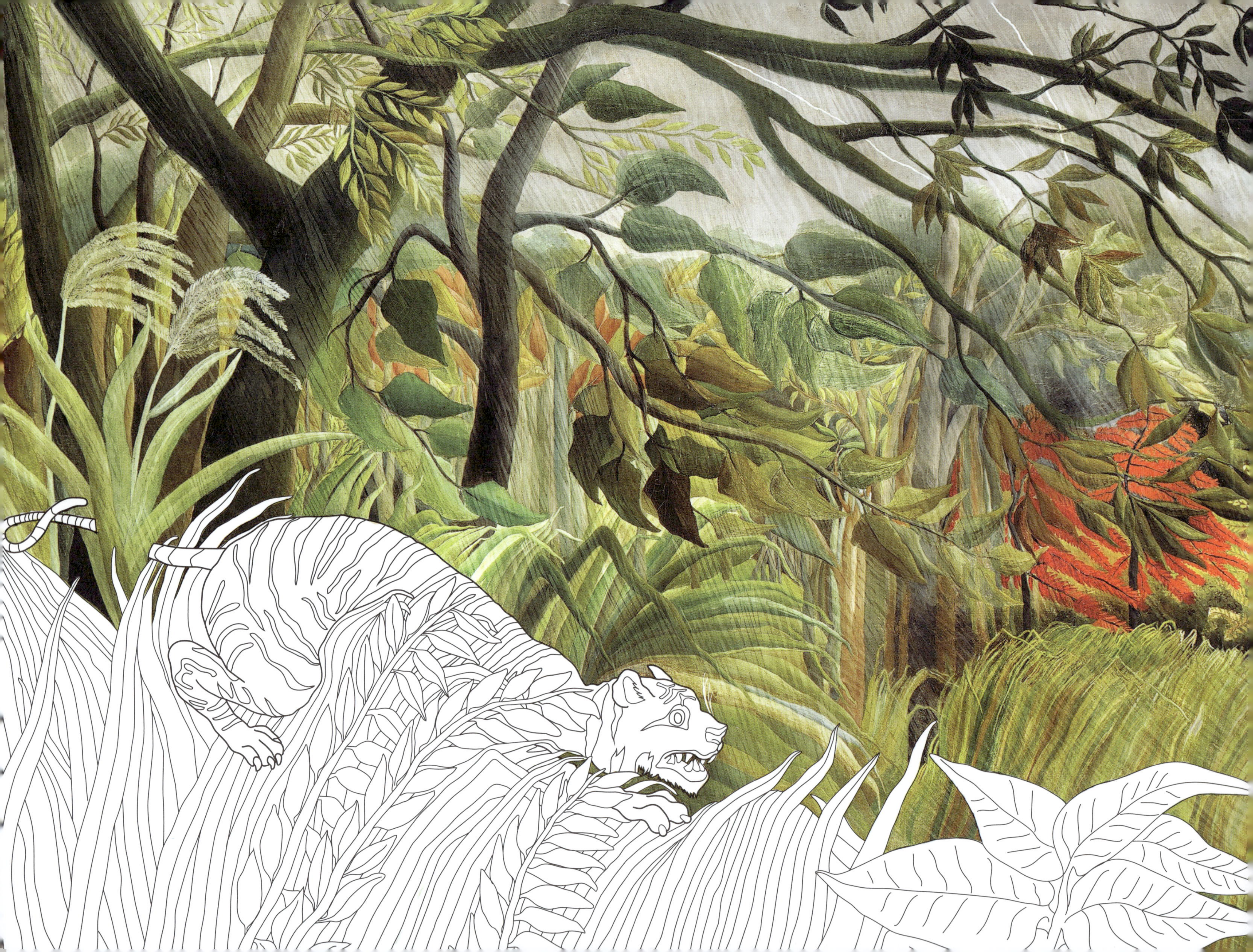

You are about to set off on a creative journey through the world of
art from Ancient Egypt and Renaissance Italy to Mughal India and
Aboriginal Australia, via Leonardo and Lichtenstein, Michelangelo and
Miró. Along the way, you'll see works by the greatest masters of art across
every style and subject, including religion and mythology, landscapes and
portraits, still lifes and battles, nature and fantasy.

However, in these pages the pictures are only outlined, waiting for your
own personal touch and embellishment. You can fill in the gaps in any way
you like: with shades close to the original, with your own preferred palette,
or by mixing and matching the masters' methods with your own. Next to
each beautifully intricate drawing is a reproduction of the original work and
a short summary of its history and meaning, so you can learn as you colour.

This book is an art studio for you to create your very own private collection,
one that no one else will ever have. So, pick up your pens, pencils and paints
and get started...

Nebamun Hunting in the Marshes
c. 1350 BCE
Unknown

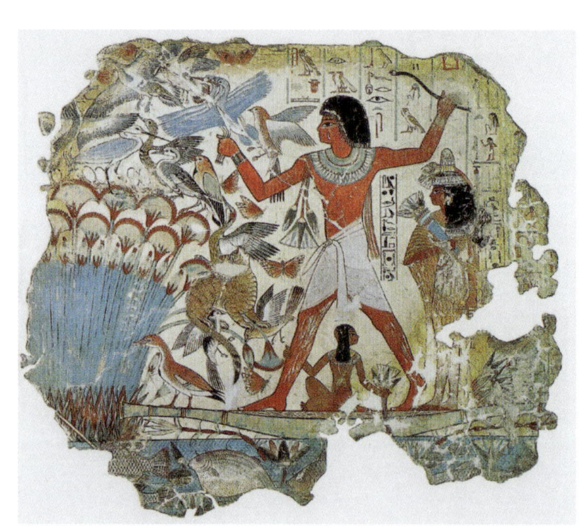

In 1820, archaeologists discovered a highly decorated tomb on the west bank of the Nile River at Thebes (now Luxor) in Egypt. It was the burial site of Nebamun, a middle-ranking official who worked in the temples sacred to the god Amun. Several of the wall paintings from the mausoleum were acquired by the British Museum in London, where they are now on display.

Traditional ancient Egyptian tomb paintings show the deceased doing what they liked to do most in life. Here we see Nebamun, his wife Hatshepsut and their young daughter in a boat hunting birds in the marshes of the Nile. The accompanying hieroglyphic states that Nebamun is 'enjoying himself and seeing beauty.'

The main colours are red and yellow ochre, both derived from local clay minerals. They are darkened by the addition of lampblack (soot), or lightened by mixing with anhydrite or huntite (white mineral sulphates of calcium and magnesium, respectively). The blues and the greens are obtained from frit, a mixture of silica and fluxes fused at high temperature. The colours are further enriched by rubbing with beeswax.

Some parts of the painting appear to have faded, but this weathered look is a deliberate attempt to depict skin seen through thin linen cloth. This effect was achieved by first applying red paint, allowing it to dry and then adding a layer of huntite, which was brushed off while still wet.

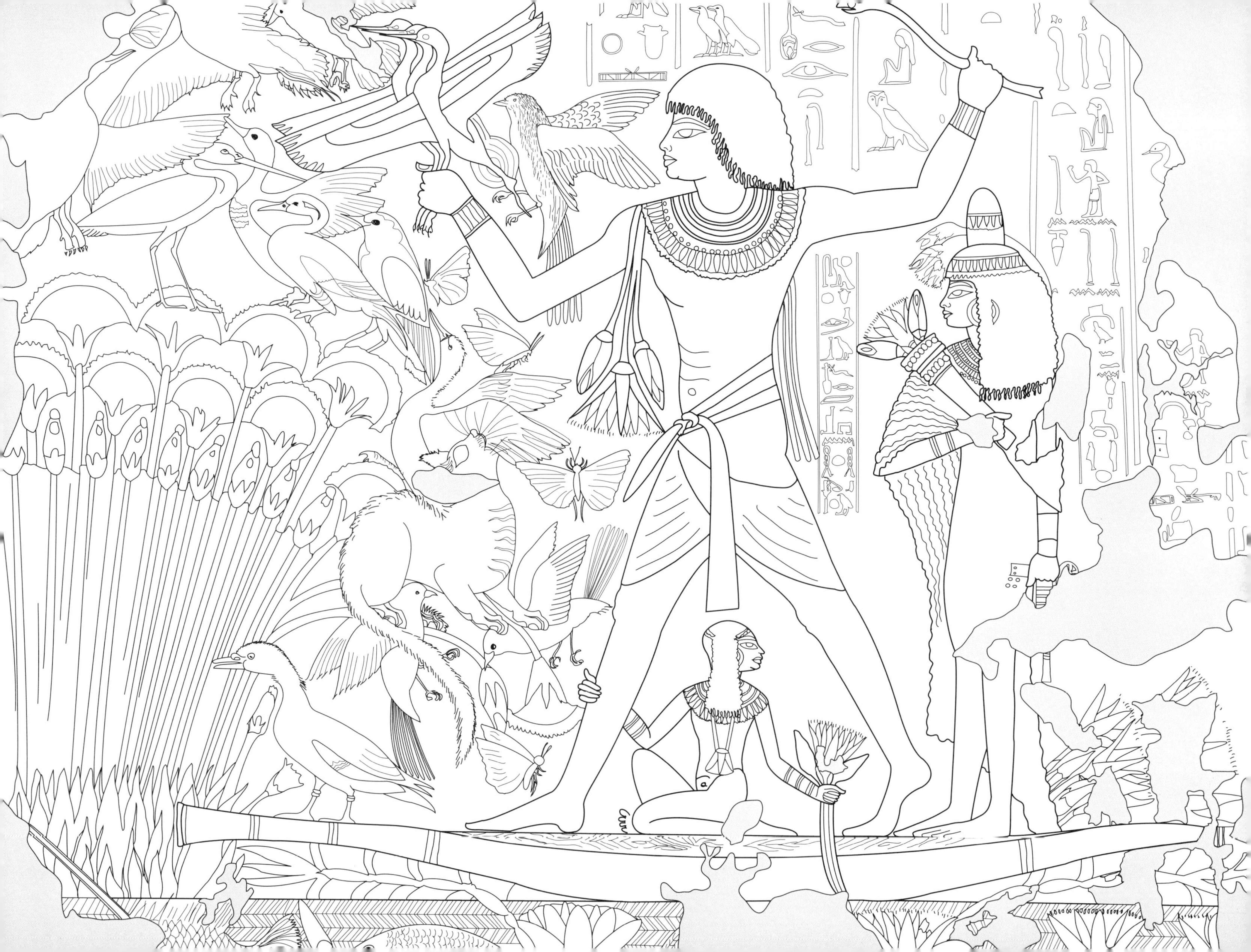

Alexander Mosaic *c.* 100 BCE

Unknown

The Alexander Mosaic originally adorned one of the floors of the House of the Faun, an opulent private residence in Pompeii, Italy. Covered in ash by the volcanic eruption of Mount Vesuvius in 79 CE, the house was excavated in 1830. A year later, this work of art was uncovered and transported to Naples, where it is now installed on a wall for ease of viewing.

The scene depicted is one of the battles between the forces of Alexander the Great and Darius III, King of Persia. There is no certainty, but it is generally believed to be the Battle of Issus (in Anatolia, modern Turkey) in 333 BCE, although some historians have suggested that the scene is the Battle of Gaugamela (in modern Iraq), which was fought two years later. In the detail opposite, Darius – seated high on his chariot – has already started to retreat; the delight in this part of the mosaic is in the detail observed in the worried expression of the Persian king, and in the Persian soldier who sees his own dying face in the reflection of his shield.

The work consists of an estimated 1.5 million pieces of stone and glass, mainly green, brown, yellow and black, none more than 4 millimetres (⅛ in.) in diameter. The pictorial narrative is so unusual for a mosaic that the work is thought to be a copy of a pre-existent painting, perhaps by Philoxenus of Eretria or Aristides of Thebes, both Greek artists of the fourth century BCE.

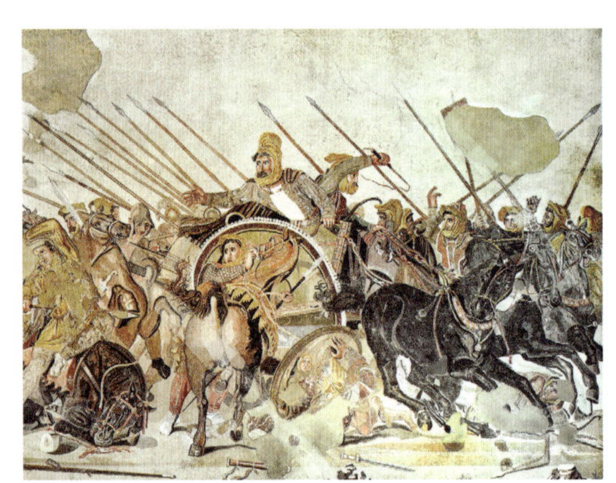

mosaic (detail)
317 cm × 555 cm
(10 ft 5 in. × 18 ft 2 ½ in.)
National Archaeological Museum, Naples

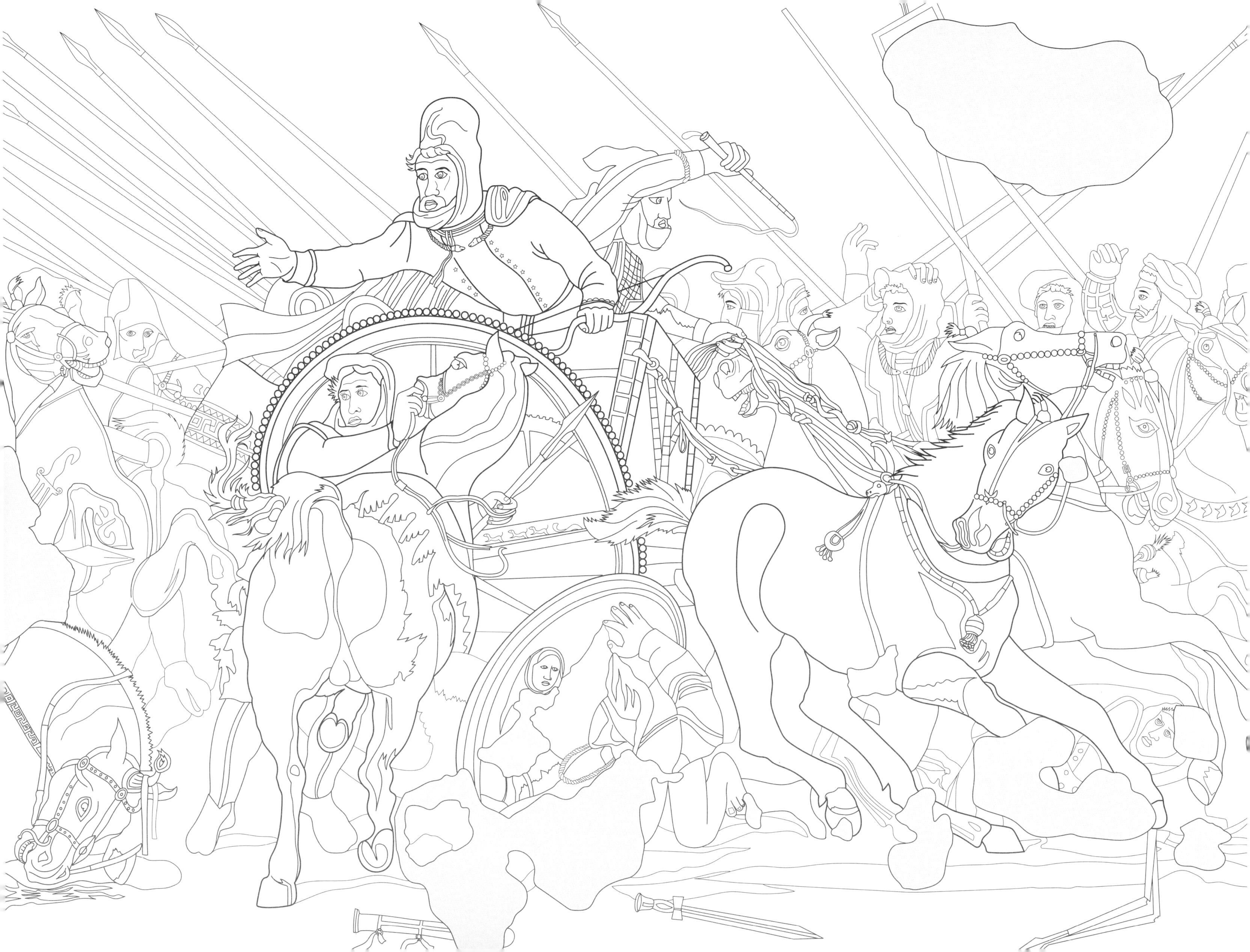

Lindisfarne Gospel c. 700 CE

Unknown

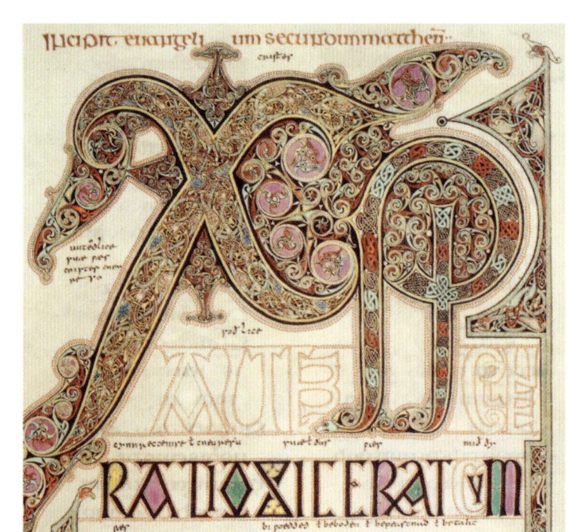

ink, pigments and gold on vellum (detail)
34.2 cm × 24.8 cm (book)
(13½ in. × 9¾ in.)
British Library, London

Irish missionary Aidan established a monastery in Lindisfarne, a small island off the coast of Northumberland in north-east England, in around 635 CE, and from there Christianity spread across the country. Produced on the island, the Lindisfarne Gospel is a manuscript containing the books of Matthew, Mark, Luke and John, which tell the story of the life of Christ in the New Testament of the Bible.

At the beginning of the Gospel according to St Matthew is an illumination that shows a monogram comprised of the first two letters – *chi* (X) and *rho* (R) – of the word 'Christ' in Greek. (The detail opposite is *rho*.) The text is executed in dense, dark brown ink and is often almost black, a tone derived from particles of carbon from soot or lampblack. However, the manuscript incorporates a wide range of animal, vegetable and mineral pigments. Some of these were derived from local sources, but others were imported from far afield: gold from the Mediterranean and blue (lapis lazuli) from the Himalayas. The colours are bound mainly by egg white, but in some places by fish glue.

It is likely that the book was made for (and could possibly have been made by) Eadfrith, the Bishop of Lindisfarne from 698 to 721. The manuscript illuminations show Irish, classical and Byzantine elements, but they are not slavish copies; they are lively and innovative originals.

Codex Zouche-Nuttall *c.* 1200 – 1521

Unknown

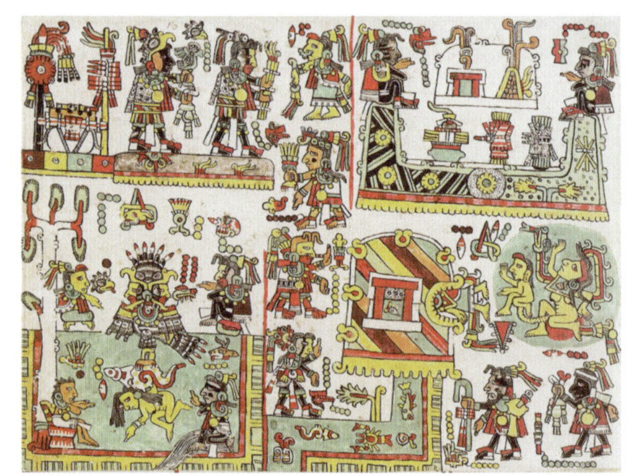

paint on deer skin (detail)
24.5 cm × 19.1 cm (page)
(9 ⅝ in. × 7 ½ in.)
British Museum, London

This is one of fewer than twenty extant manuscripts from Central America that pre-date the Spanish conquest of the region, which began in 1519. It was produced by the Mixtecs, a Native American people who occupied an area roughly equivalent to that of the modern Mexican state of Oaxaca.

This Codex (screenfold book) comprises forty-seven deerskin leaves that measure a total of 11 metres (36 ft) in length. Two narratives are featured: on the side shown opposite is the history of important Mixtec centres; on the other side is the genealogy, life and military achievements of Iya Nacuaa Teyusi Ñaña (Eight Deer Jaguar Claw), the Mixtec ruler who became a human sacrifice in around 1115. Interestingly, the two sides of the Codex differ stylistically, which suggests that it was the work of at least two people. Both sides use similar colours, such as light and dark red, blue, purple, black and grey. However, green and light yellow appear only on the front, whereas dark yellow is used only on the back.

It is not entirely clear how the manuscript reached Europe, but in 1859 it turned up in a monastery in Florence, Italy. Shortly afterwards, it was acquired by the English aristocrat Sir Robert Curzon, Baron Zouche, and it was published in 1902 by Zelia Nuttall, an American anthropologist – hence its name. The Curzon family first lent it, and later donated it, to the British Museum in London.

The Battle of San Romano c. 1438 – 40

Paolo Uccello c. 1397 – 1475

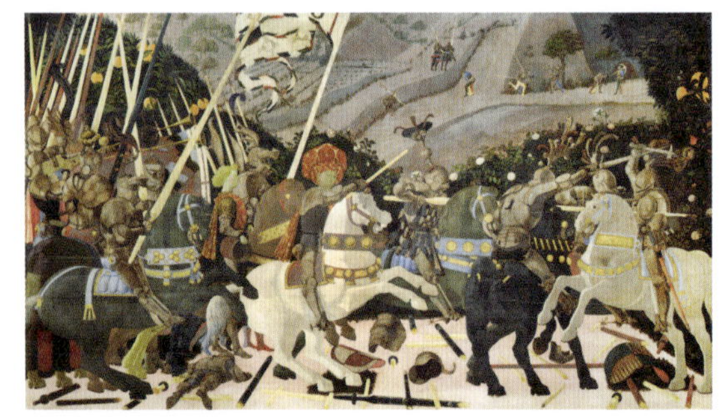

egg tempera with walnut oil and linseed oil on poplar
182 cm × 320 cm (panel)
(71 ⅝ in. × 10 ft 6 in.)
National Gallery, London

Paolo di Dono was a Florentine artist who is known by the name Paolo
Uccello because of his early fame as a painter of wildlife (*uccello* is Italian
for 'bird'). Today, he is recognized as one of the great early masters of
Renaissance perspective.

The Battle of San Romano is Uccello's best-known painting and is a triptych
portraying different scenes from the same battle. Shown here is the panel that
depicts the victory of the Florentine forces over those of Siena in a minor
confrontation of 1432. It is known as 'the London panel' to distinguish it
from the others located in Paris and Florence. In addition to its technical
brilliance, the painting's greatness lies in the inspired combination of Gothic
decorative patterns with the sculptured forms of the Renaissance. This
section shows Florentine commander Niccolò da Tolentino, backed by only
twenty soldiers, surprising the Sienese. It is an impressive example of war
imagery and demonstrates Uccello's fascination with perspective; an array
of splintered spears, strewn bodies and colourful heraldic armour leads the
viewer through an exhilarating display of violence and bloodthirsty chaos.

The whiteness of the commander's horse is enhanced by its contrast with
the surrounding colours: black, greyish brown, creamy white, pale to golden
yellow, light royal blue, greyish blue-green and pinkish brown to reddish
brown. Niccolò's skin is olive green.

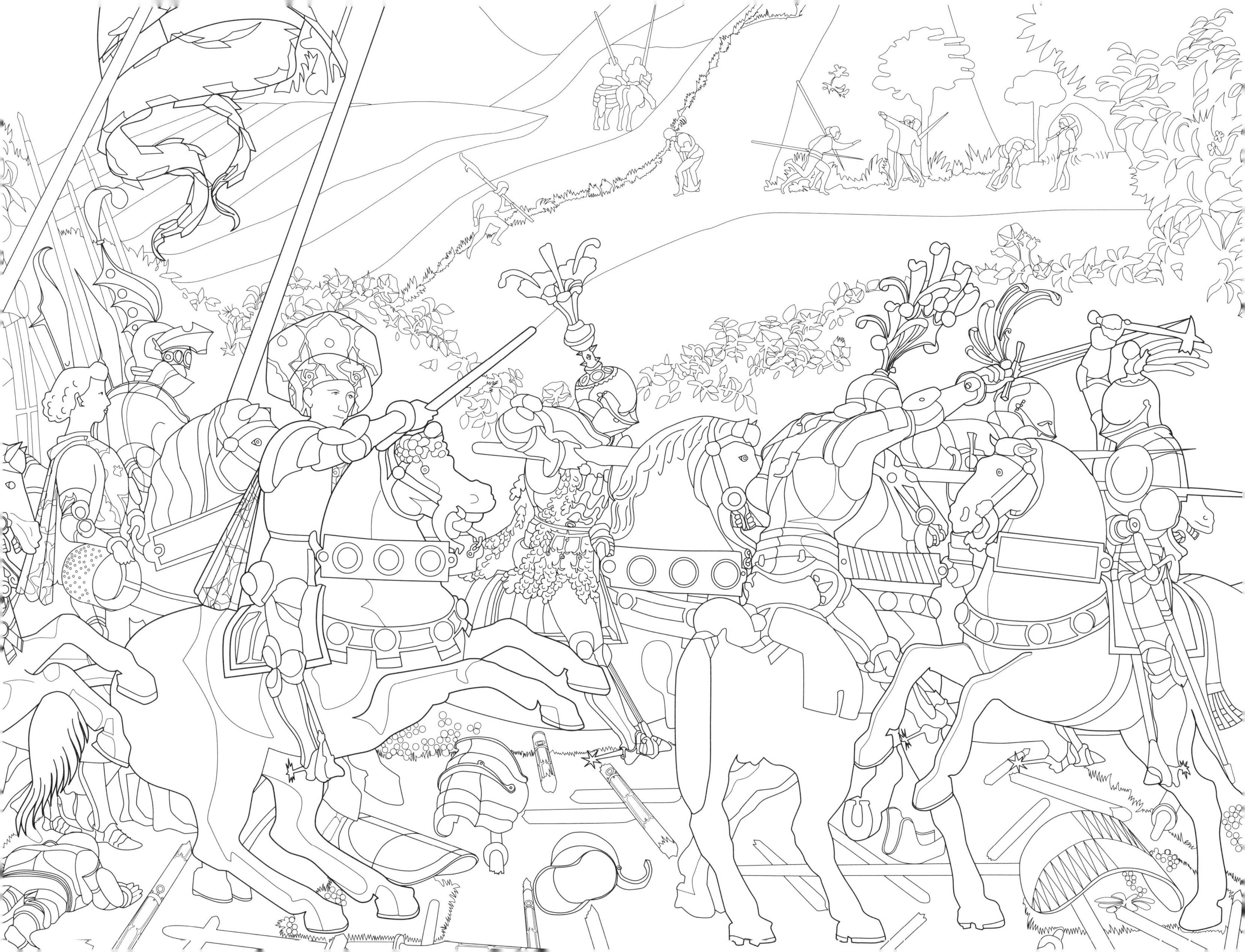

Annunciation c. 1472

Leonardo da Vinci 1452 – 1519

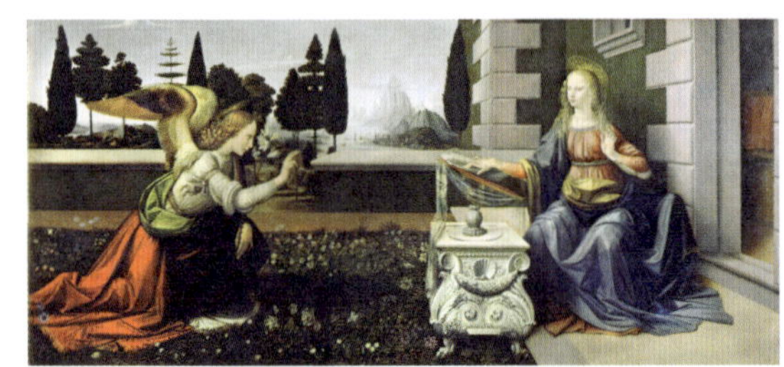

oil and tempera on wood panel
98 cm × 217 cm
(38 ½ in. × 85 ⅜ in.)
Uffizi, Florence

Born in the city of Vinci in what is now Italy, Leonardo da Vinci was a versatile genius who excelled in architecture, drawing, engineering and sculpture, as well as in oil painting. In this early biblical canvas, which was a partial collaboration with his teacher Andrea del Verrocchio, the archangel Gabriel appears before the Virgin Mary to tell her that she will give birth to Jesus Christ, the Son of God.

The foreground colours are intense, and the draperies and clothing – the angel's red robes, Mary's blue skirts – are richly detailed. This section of the canvas contrasts strikingly with the cool and sombre shades of olive green used for the trees, and their gradual transition into the grey-white of the distant mountain. However, this is not to suggest that the foreground and background areas of the composition do not belong together. On the contrary, each element of the painting informs and echoes its other parts: indeed, Gabriel's message bag connects the foreground to the background, and the Madonna lily that he holds in his left hand is a counterpoint to the distant snowy peak. This flower is also a symbol of both virginity and the city of Florence, in which the masterpiece was created. The Virgin's pose and expression convey that she has been taken by surprise, as does the position in which she holds her right hand, appearing to reserve her place in the Scripture.

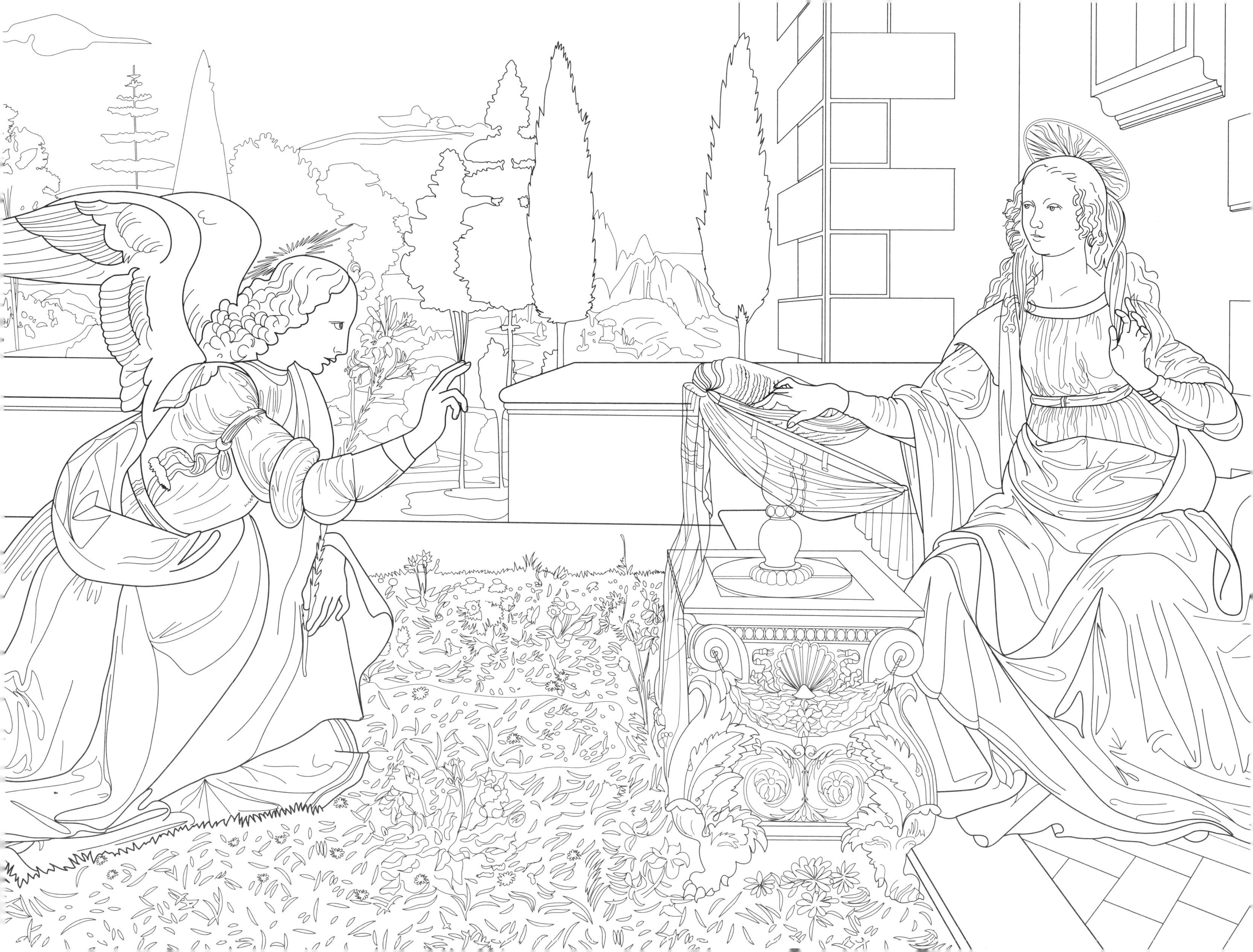

Primavera c. 1478

Sandro Botticelli 1445 – 1510

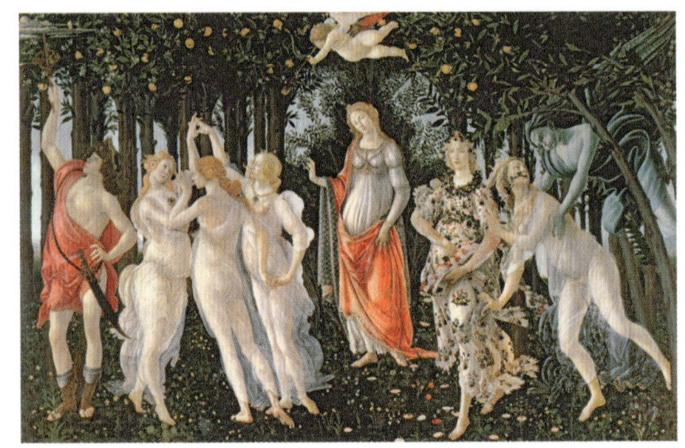

tempera on wood panel
175.5 cm × 278.5 cm
(69 in. × 9 ft 1 in.)
Uffizi, Florence

After training as a goldsmith, Sandro Botticelli served as an apprentice to Fra Filippo Lippi, who expertly portrayed expressive interactions between figures and was a master of decorative detailing. He was also influenced by Antonio Pollaiuolo, who depicted human anatomy with a realism that was unusual at the time. Apart from a year spent in Rome painting the wall frescoes of the Sistine Chapel in the Vatican, Botticelli lived the whole of his life in Florence.

Primavera (Spring) – a title supplied forty years after Botticelli's death by Giorgio Vasari, author of *Lives of the Artists* (1550) – depicts a lively scene featuring, from left to right, Mercury, the messenger of the gods; the Three Graces (Euphrosyne, Aglaia and Thalia); Venus, the goddess of love; Flora, the goddess of fecundity; the nymph Chloris; and Zephyr, the west wind. Above them, Cupid, the god of erotic love, aims his dart at the Three Graces.

The painting is framed at the top by a grove of orange trees, which forms a canopy above the figures, and at the base by the petals strewn on a carpet of grass. Mercury and Venus, whose clothes, although different in hue, are both shades of red, attract the viewer's immediate attention. Elsewhere, the flowers on Flora's dress and in her hands are a riot of pinks and reds. The delicate attire of the other five standing figures and of Cupid's wings are depicted in varying shades of white.

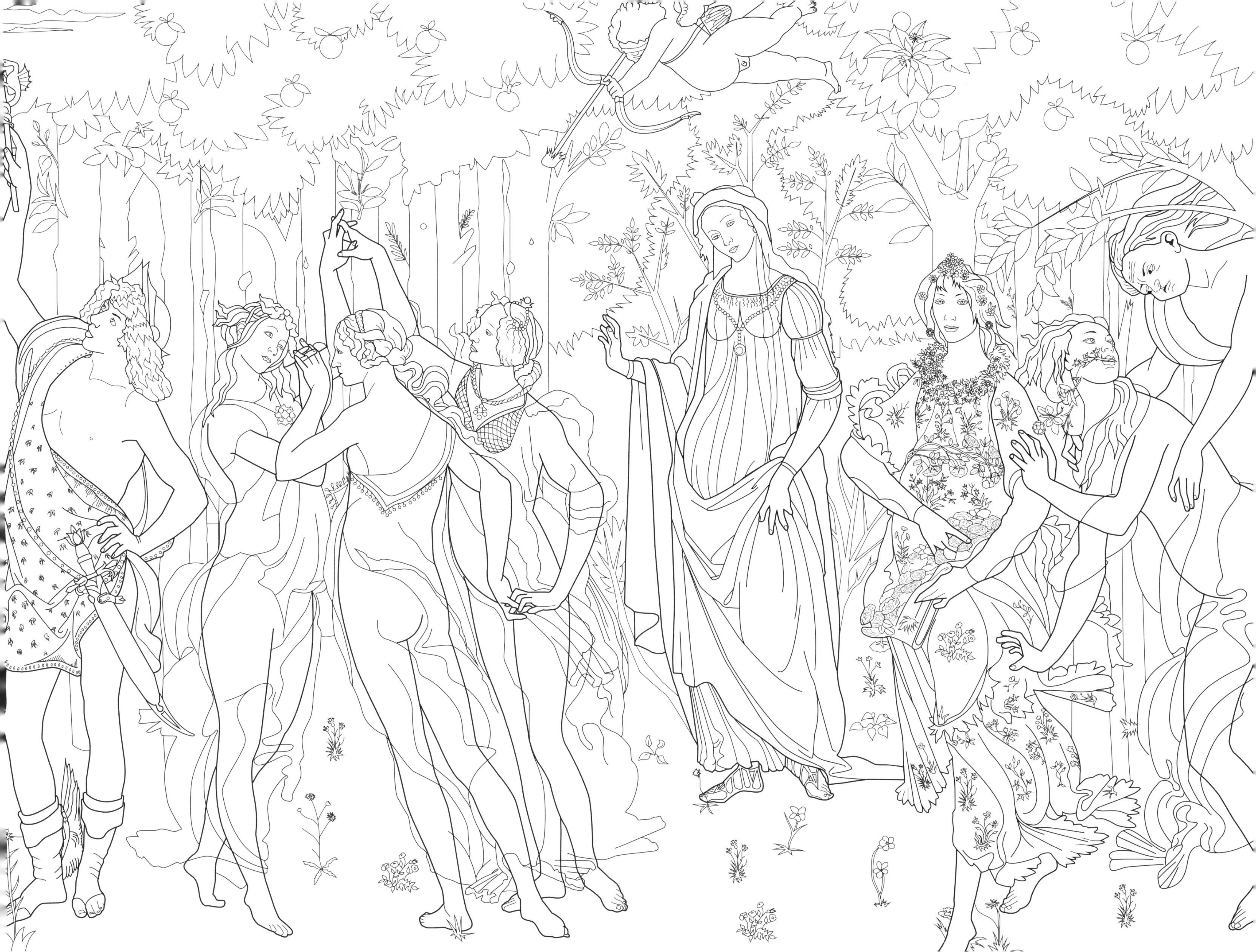

The Lady and the Unicorn *c.* 1500

Unknown

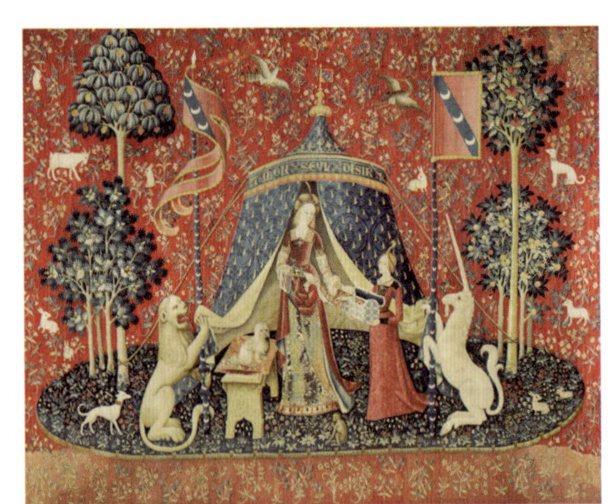

wool and silk (detail)
369 cm × 473 cm
(12 ft 1 in. × 15 ft 6 in.)
Musée National du Moyen Âge, Paris

The Lady and the Unicorn is the informal title of a series of six tapestries woven in Flanders for a noble French family. Each cloth features a woman with a unicorn on her left and a lion on her right, in different settings. Five of the tapestries are believed to be allegorical representations of the senses; they are displayed in order, from the most elemental to the most refined: touch (the woman holds the unicorn's horn and a flag); taste (she feeds a bird); smell (she holds flowers); hearing (she plays music); and sight (she shows the unicorn his reflection in a mirror).

The sixth tapestry, shown here, is named À *mon seul désir* (To my only desire). It depicts the woman inside the parting folds of a tent, held open by the lion and the unicorn. The precise meaning of both the scene and the title is unclear. Some people believe that the image represents the heart, the sixth sense; others think that it shows the woman renouncing the passions aroused by the senses depicted in the other five tapestries.

All six tapestries are woven in the millefleurs style, which means that their backgrounds are made up of numerous small flowers and plants. The works were lost for hundreds of years until 1841, when French author Prosper Mérimée rediscovered them in the Château de Boussac in Limousin, France. George Sand featured the tapestries in her novel *Jeanne* (1844) and they are central to Tracy Chevalier's novel *The Lady and the Unicorn* (2003).

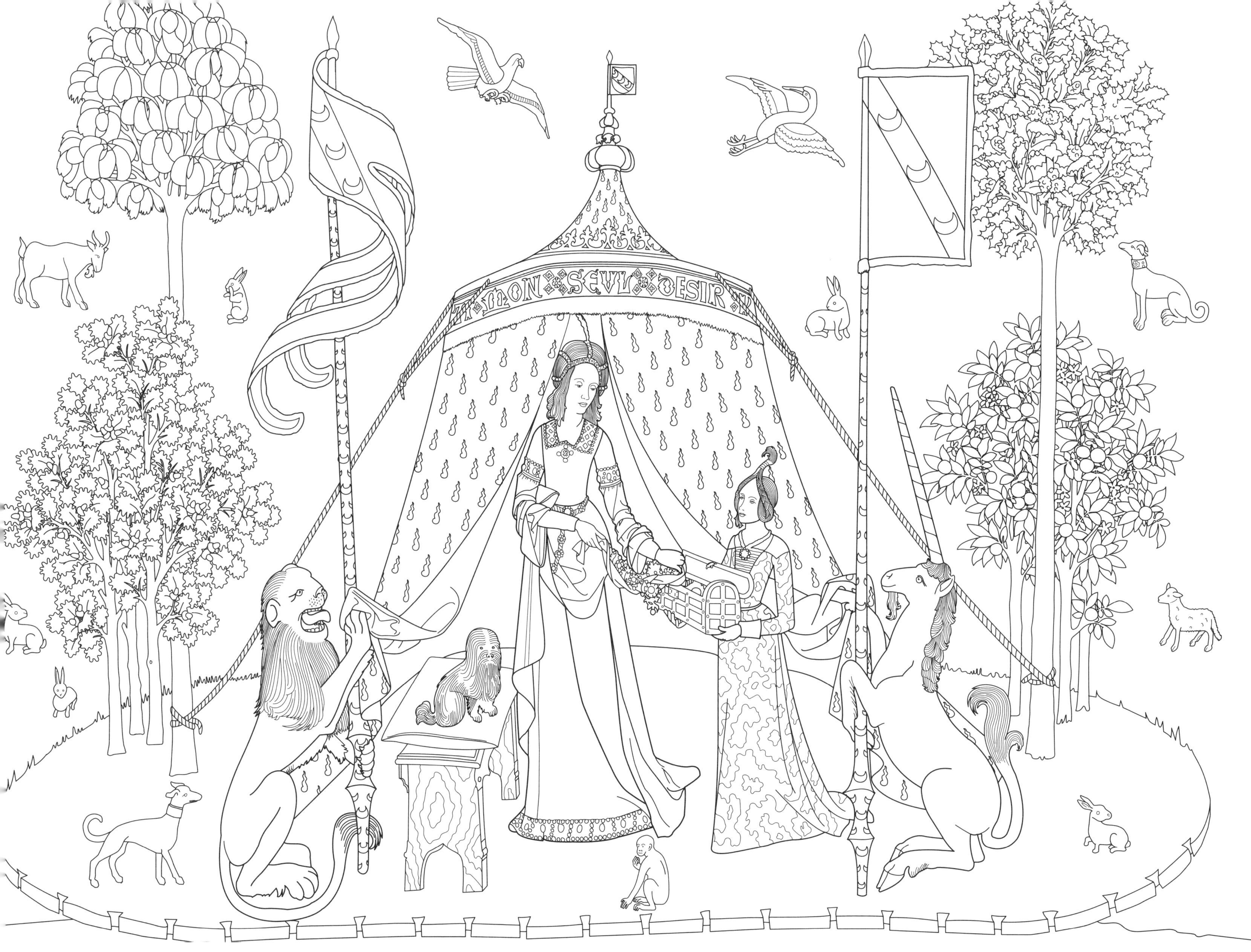

MON SEVL DESIR

Madonna of the Meadow c. 1505

Raphael 1483–1520

One of the greatest painters and architects of the Italian High Renaissance, Raphael (Raffaello Sanzio da Urbino) was born in Urbino. He became a leading member of the Florentine school of art and then moved to Rome, where he made a major contribution to the reconstruction of St Peter's Basilica.

Madonna of the Meadow depicts Mary, Mother of God, supporting the baby Jesus, who is evidently close to walking unaided. Kneeling before the Christ child is John the Baptist. He looks intently at Jesus and holds up a miniature cross, which Jesus clasps in one hand while gently holding his mother's arm with the other. There is plenty of religious symbolism in this painting, both in the composition and the colours. For example, the contact points between the three figures and the clear delineation of humans, land and sky into three separate layers allude to the Holy Trinity (God the Father, God the Son and God the Holy Spirit). These layers are crossed by the Madonna, whose depiction sweeps diagonally across the canvas and unites every element, both visually and theologically.

The rich blue of the Madonna's gold-trimmed mantle represents the Church and her red dress symbolizes the blood of Christ, which will be shed in the sacrifice that brings salvation to humankind. The poppies to one side refer to death and resurrection.

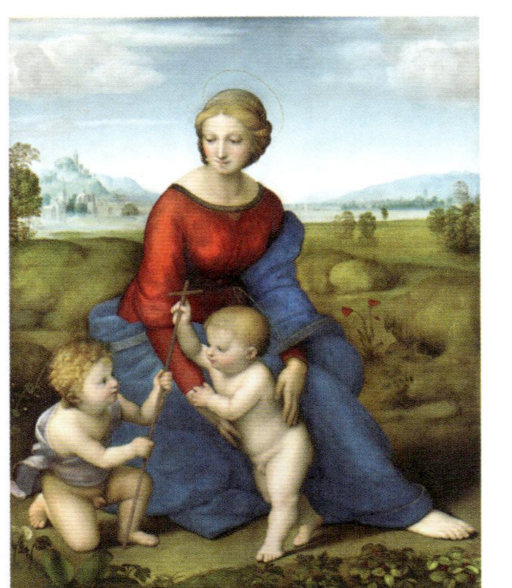

oil on board
113 cm × 88 cm
(44 ½ in. × 34 ⅝ in.)
Kunsthistorisches Museum, Vienna

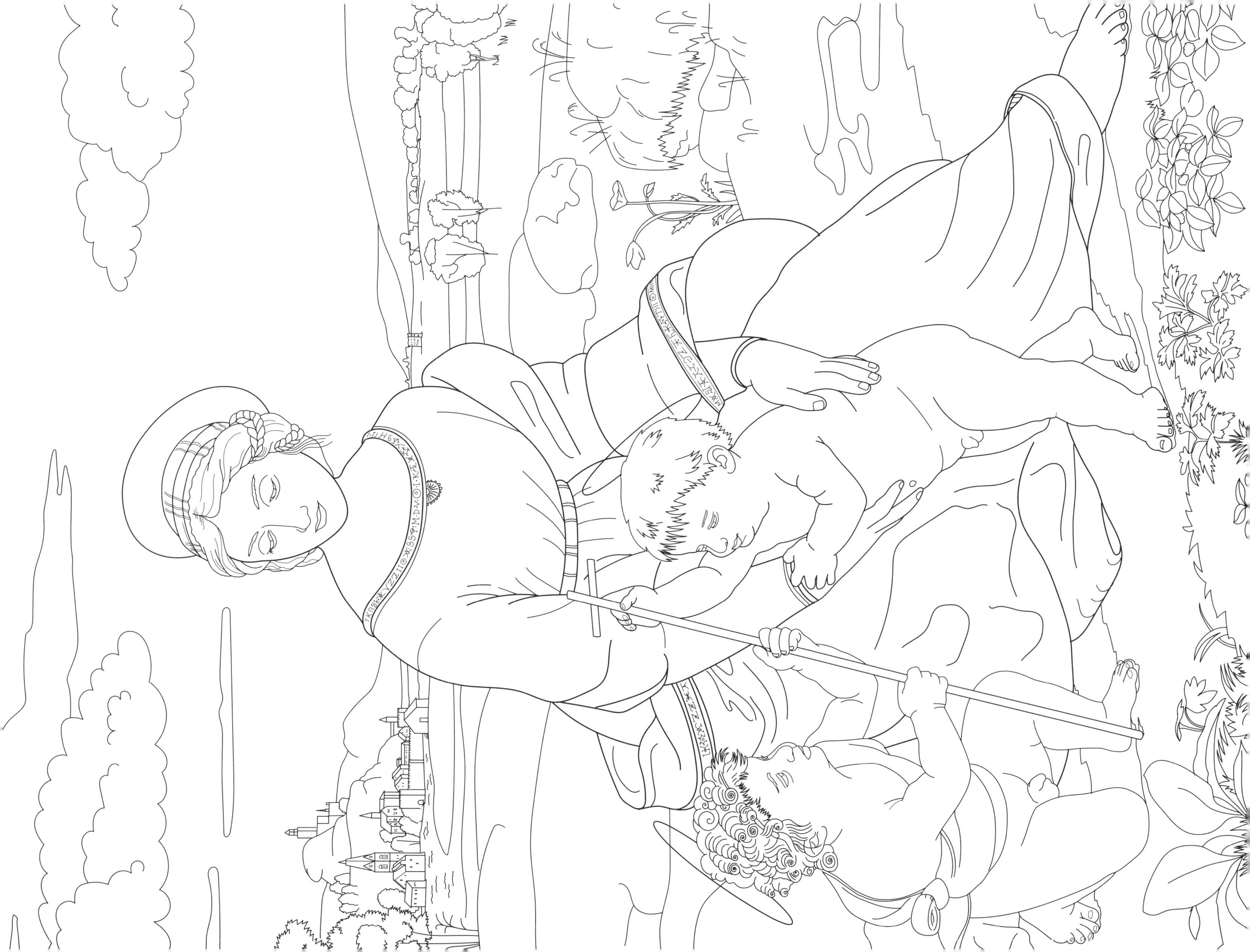

Creation of Adam c. 1512

Michelangelo 1475–1564

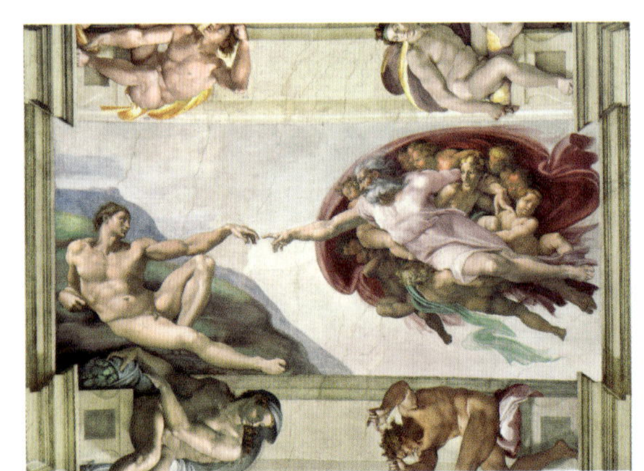

fresco
280 cm × 570 cm (detail)
(9 ft 2 in. × 18 ft 8 in.)
Sistine Chapel, Vatican City

One of the greatest and most versatile artists of all time, Michelangelo Buonarroti was a sculptor, painter, architect, draughtsman and poet who worked between Florence, Bologna and Rome. The entire ceiling fresco of the Vatican's Sistine Chapel – of which the detail shown here is the best-known section – measures 40 by 14 metres (131 x 46 ft) and it was commissioned by Pope Julius II in 1508. Initially, Michelangelo was reluctant to take on the project, because he saw himself primarily as a sculptor. But it came to dominate his life, and he spent four years single-handedly painting it, during which time his style evolved.

Michelangelo's knowledge of anatomy and his sculptural skill are evident in many of the poses of the figures, which pay tribute to classical Greek and Roman sculpture. He made some 300 preliminary drawings – known as cartoons – which were then enlarged and transferred to the ceiling. His sculptural thinking led him to abandon scenic detail in order to focus on the gesture and movement of the figures.

On the right of the painting, God is wearing a milky-white tunic. He and the surrounding figures, one of which may be Eve or the Virgin Mary, are encased in a warm brown shape that resembles a human brain. On the left, the dominant greens and blue suggest a chill that will be banished when God's outstretched finger touches Adam and gives life to humanity.

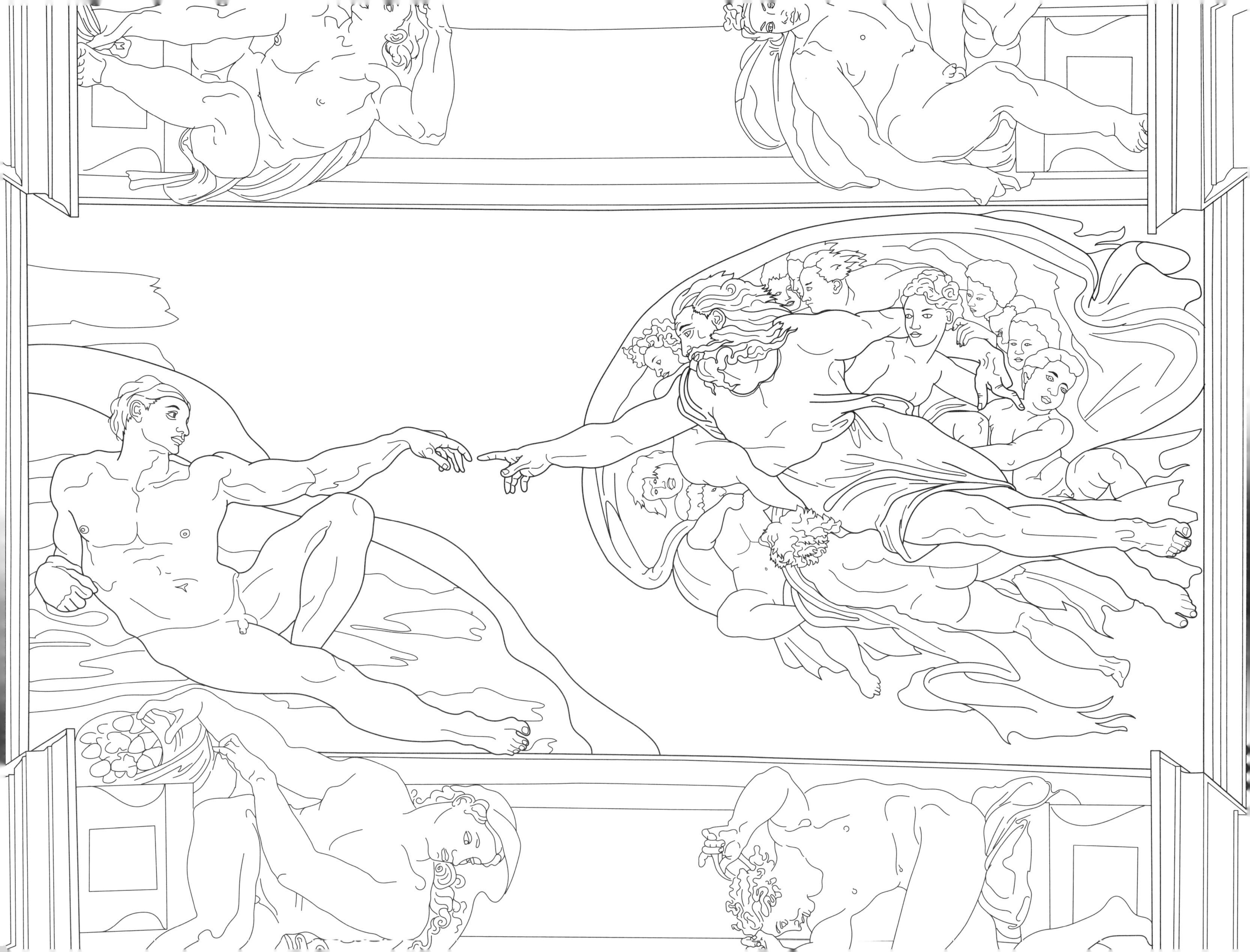

Melencolia I 1514

Albrecht Dürer 1471–1528

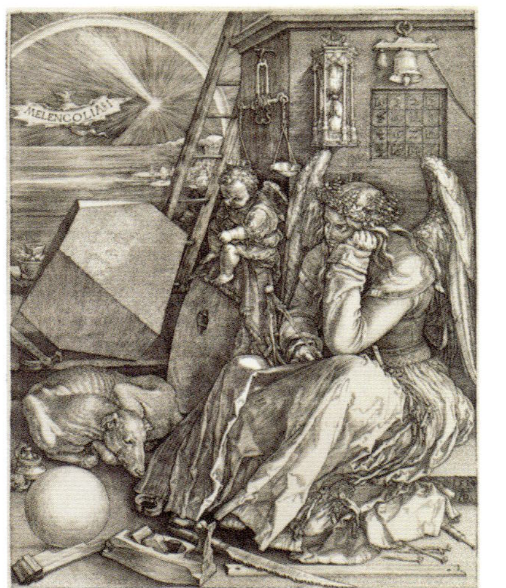

engraving
24 cm × 18.8 cm
(9 ⅜ in. × 7 ⅜ in.)
Graphische Sammlung, Munich

Born and raised in Nuremberg, Germany, Albrecht Dürer was a painter and engraver who first brought the styles of the Renaissance to northern Europe. *Melencolia I* shows a winged female holding a pair of dividers and surrounded by various tools associated with art, craft, mathematics and science. Her eyes are piercing and strongly suggest a keen intelligence, but her pose – elbow on knee, head on hand – is a well-established indication of sadness. The nature of her mood is shown clearly in the banner held by the bat-like being in the top left corner of the picture.

Medieval physicians believed that there were four humours, or moods: sanguine (optimistic and social), choleric (short-tempered and irritable), phlegmatic (relaxed and peaceful) and melancholic (analytical and quiet). An excess of any one of these would cause sickness, and too much black bile caused melancholy, the state of mind that makes sufferers inactive and prevents them from finishing anything. Modern medical practitioners would call this depression. One of Dürer's great influences, Leonardo da Vinci, was known to have suffered from depression, and although his output was prolific, he left numerous projects uncompleted. The outline below can be coloured in, or perhaps more of a challenge would be to use varying shades of grey pencil.

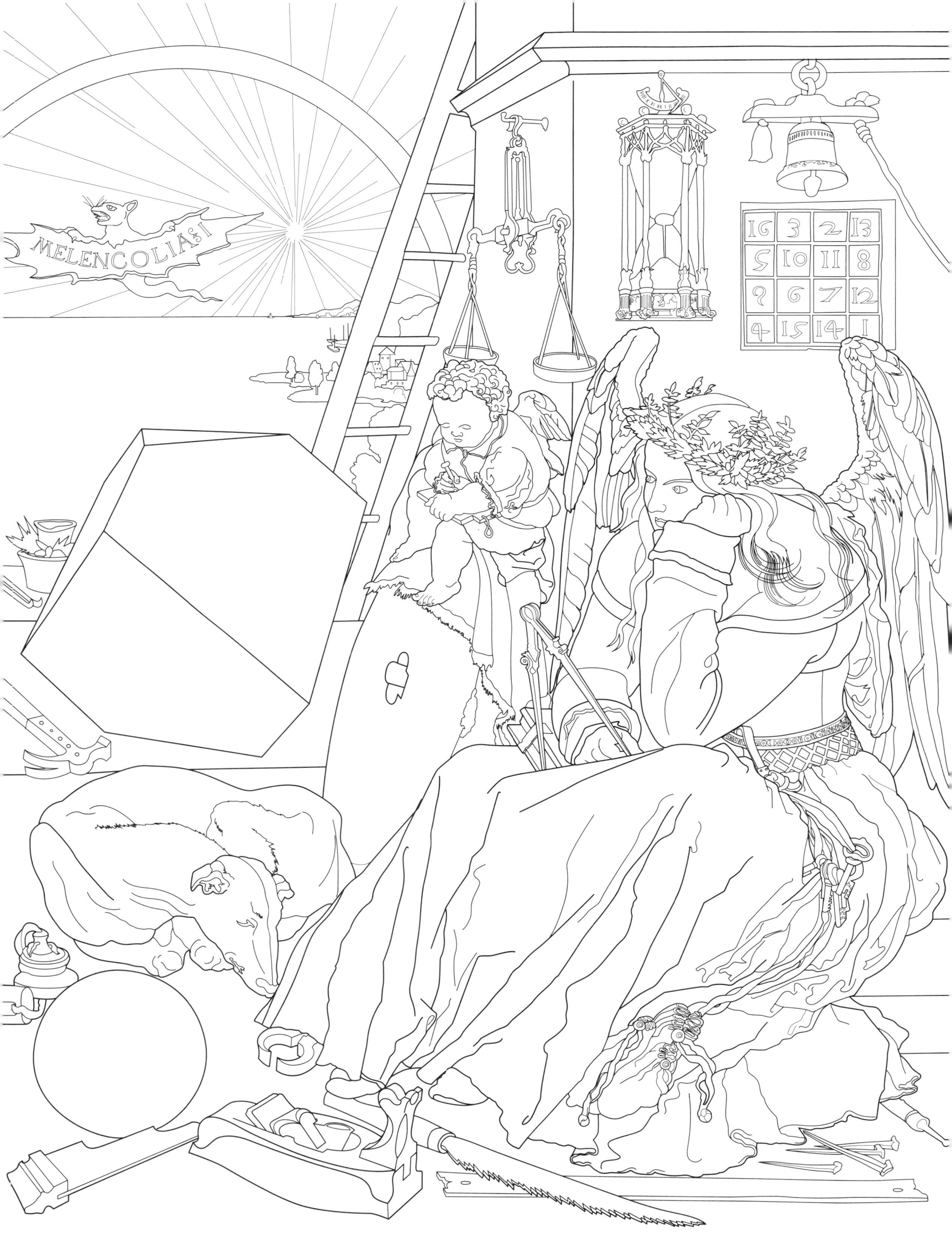

MELENCOLIA § I

Bacchus and Ariadne 1520 – 23

Titian *c.* 1488 – 1576

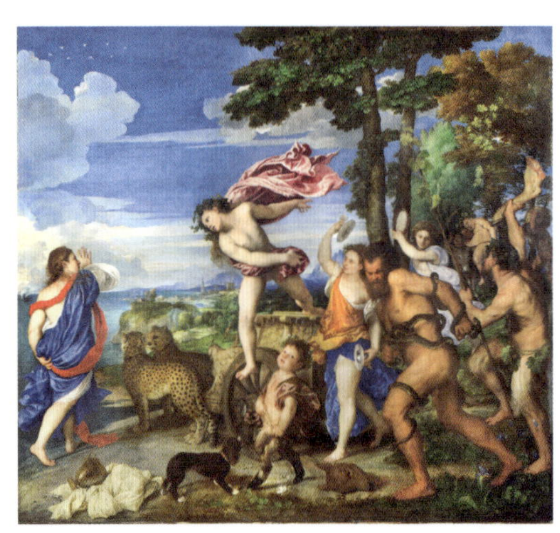

oil on canvas
176.5 cm × 191 cm
(69½ in. × 75 in.)
National Gallery, London

Born in a village in the mountains to the north of Venice, Titian (Tiziano Vecellio) was sent to the city at the age of ten to study painting under Giovanni Bellini. After Bellini's death in 1516, Titian was given the job of finishing his old master's outstanding commissions. He was also given work that had been assigned to Raphael, such as this painting, after the latter's death in 1520.

Bacchus and Ariadne depicts a classical myth and illustrates the first encounter between Bacchus, the god of wine, and Ariadne, the daughter of Minos, King of Crete. Here, Bacchus enters the scene from the landscape to the right, riding a chariot drawn by two cheetahs and leading a lively band of followers. On the left of the canvas is Ariadne, who has been abandoned on the Greek island of Naxos by her lover, Theseus; his departing ship can just be seen sailing away in the distance. For Bacchus, this is love at first sight and he leaps towards his future bride. Ariadne fears him at first, but Titian shows that all will end well by including a circle of stars above her head. This is a reference to the end of the story, in which Ariadne is raised to Heaven and turned into a constellation.

The sky is rendered in a deep blue pigment known as ultramarine, which was rare and costly at the time; its liberal use confirms that money was no object at this stage of Titian's career.

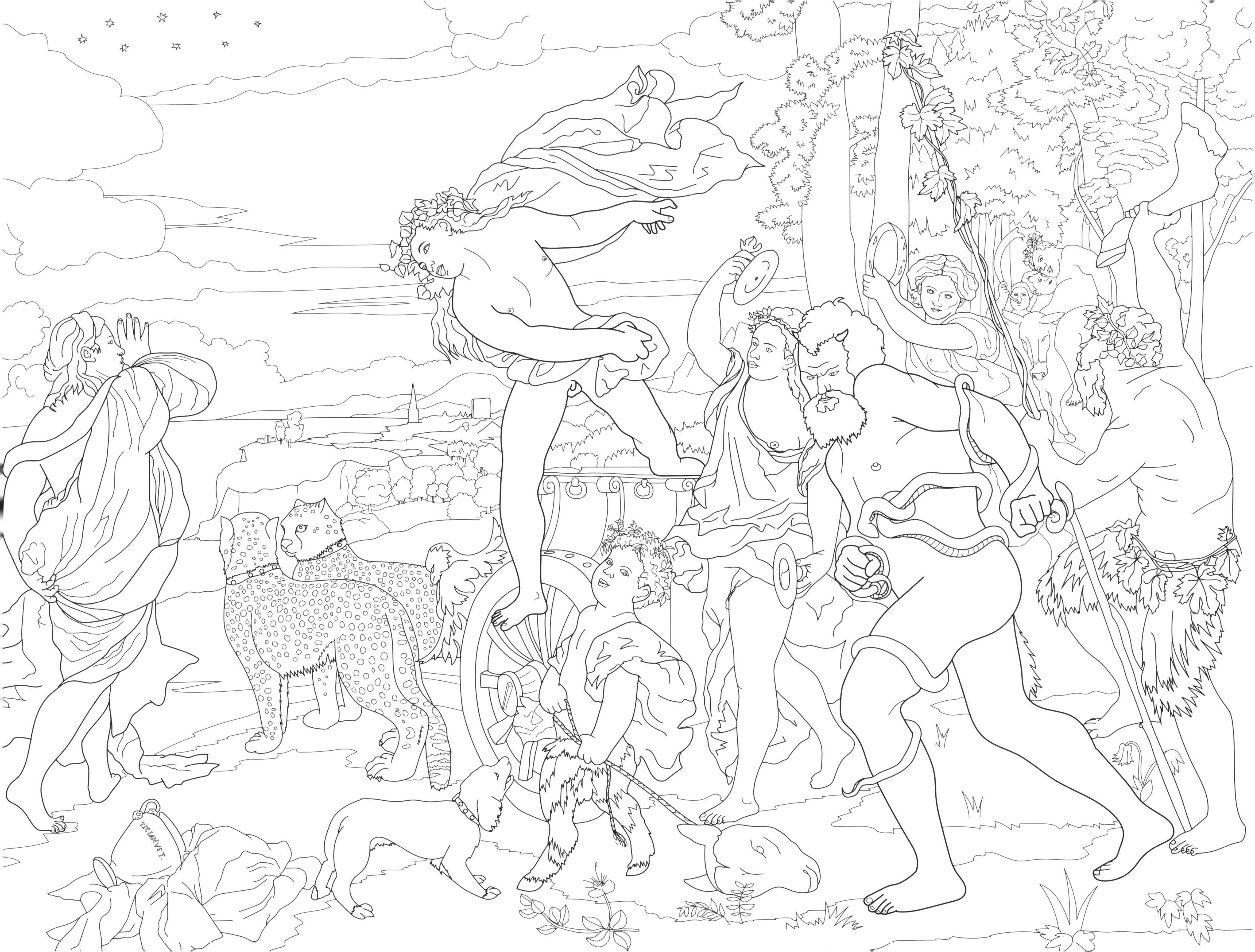

The Ambassadors 1533

Hans Holbein the Younger c. 1497–1543

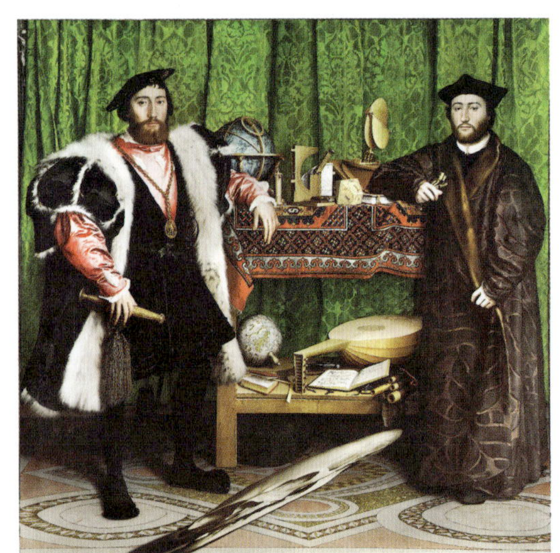

oil on oak panel
207 cm × 209 cm
(81 ½ in. × 82 ½ in.)
National Gallery, London

Born in Augsburg, Germany, Hans Holbein the Younger made his career in England, painting portraits of members of and visitors to the court of King Henry VIII. This full-length double portrait shows two French courtiers: Jean de Dinteville (on the left), ambassador to England, and Georges de Selve, a cleric. The objects laid out between them include navigational, astrological and musical instruments, a sundial (showing the date 11 April 1533) and a hymn book. These items reflect the men's interests, but the canvas is also full of hidden meanings.

The painting celebrates human achievement and wealth, especially in its opulent colours: the green of the background wall covering, the reds of the cloth over the table and de Dinteville's shirt, the gold of his necklace and the white of his fur coat lining. However, Holbein is also reminding us that worldly success is ultimately meaningless because no matter what we achieve, we all must die. The broken lute string, for example, is a traditional symbol of death and it may also refer to the Protestant split from the Church of Rome, something that the ambassadors were trying to prevent. Many portraits from this period contain an image of a skull as a memento mori, but none is more unusual than the one in the foreground here. Holbein has distorted the perspective so that the skull becomes apparent only when the painting is viewed from the right-hand side.

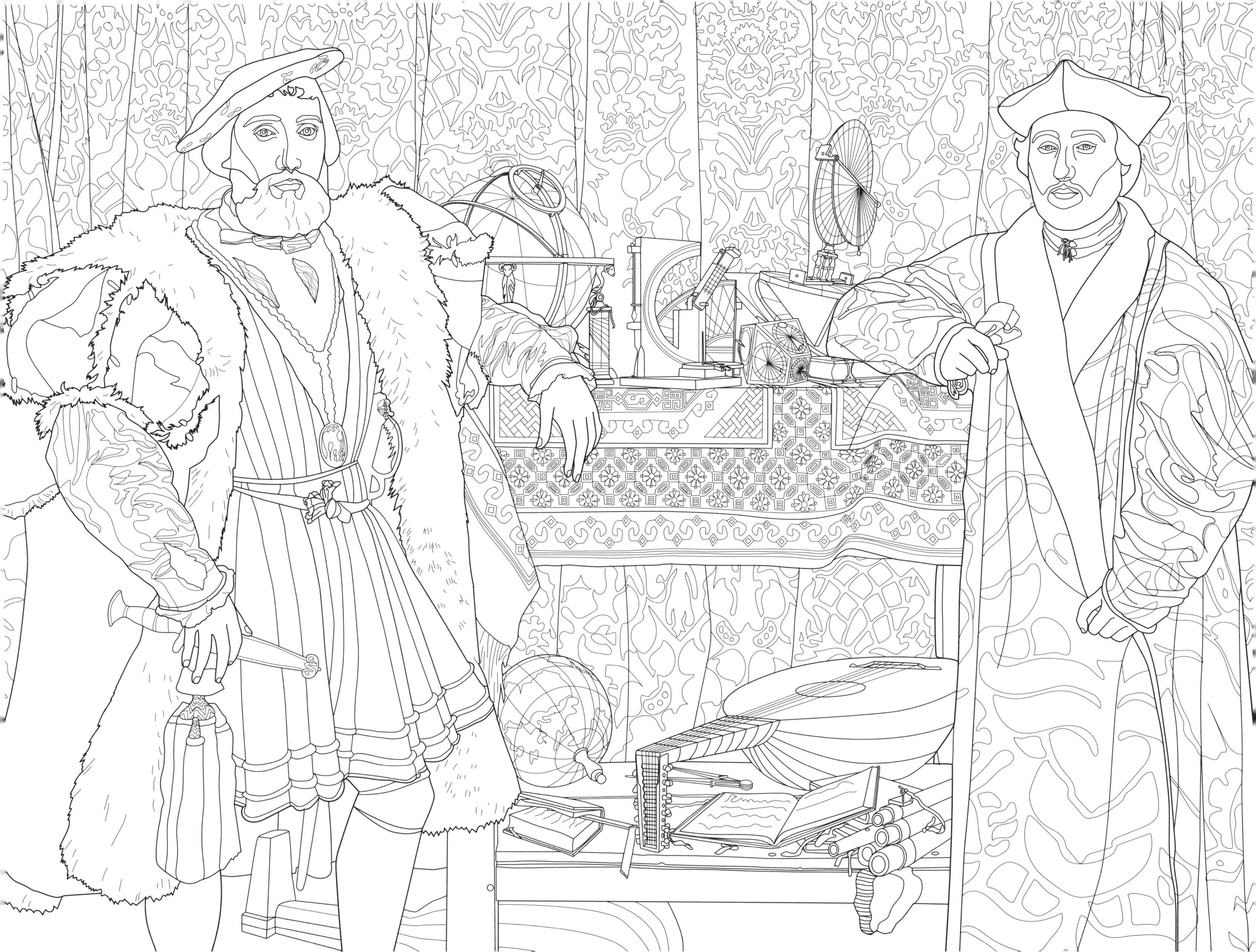

Hunters in the Snow 1565

Pieter Bruegel the Elder c. 1525 – 1569

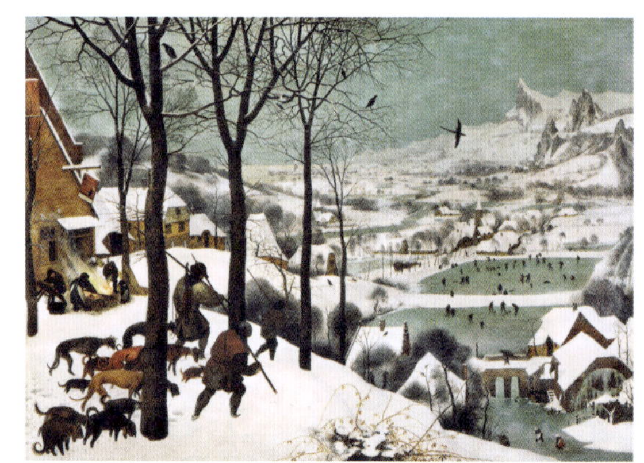

oil on wood panel
117 cm × 162 cm
(46 in. × 63¾ in.)
Kunsthistorisches Museum, Vienna

The first in a family of Flemish painters, Pieter Bruegel the Elder specialized
in landscapes and narrative depictions of peasant life focused on trials
and hardships. This painting was originally part of a series, *Months*,
commissioned by Nicolaes Jonghelinck, a wealthy banker from Antwerp.
It probably represents January. This can be deduced from the scene
on the left, in which villagers are preparing to singe a pig to remove its
bristles. Among the other surviving paintings in the series are *The Gloomy
Day* (February), *Haymaking* (July), *The Harvesters* (August) and *The Return
of the Herd* (perhaps November).

The line of trees is a framing device, and the direction of the huntsmen
and their dogs leads the eye to the centre of the canvas. Although Bruegel
paid great attention to minute details – the tiny figures skating, tobogganing
and curling on the ice are particular joys – this painting does not show
an accurate view of a specific place. Instead, it is a composite scene. The
mountains in the distance are based on sketches that the artist made from
1552 to 1553, when he travelled through the Alps on his way to Italy; the rest
of the panorama was inspired by the flat terrain of Holland and Belgium.

The colour scheme is appropriate for a cold, gloomy afternoon in winter:
pale green sky and ice, and less-than-pure white snow, offset against the
dark browns and blacks of the trees, birds, dogs and human figures.

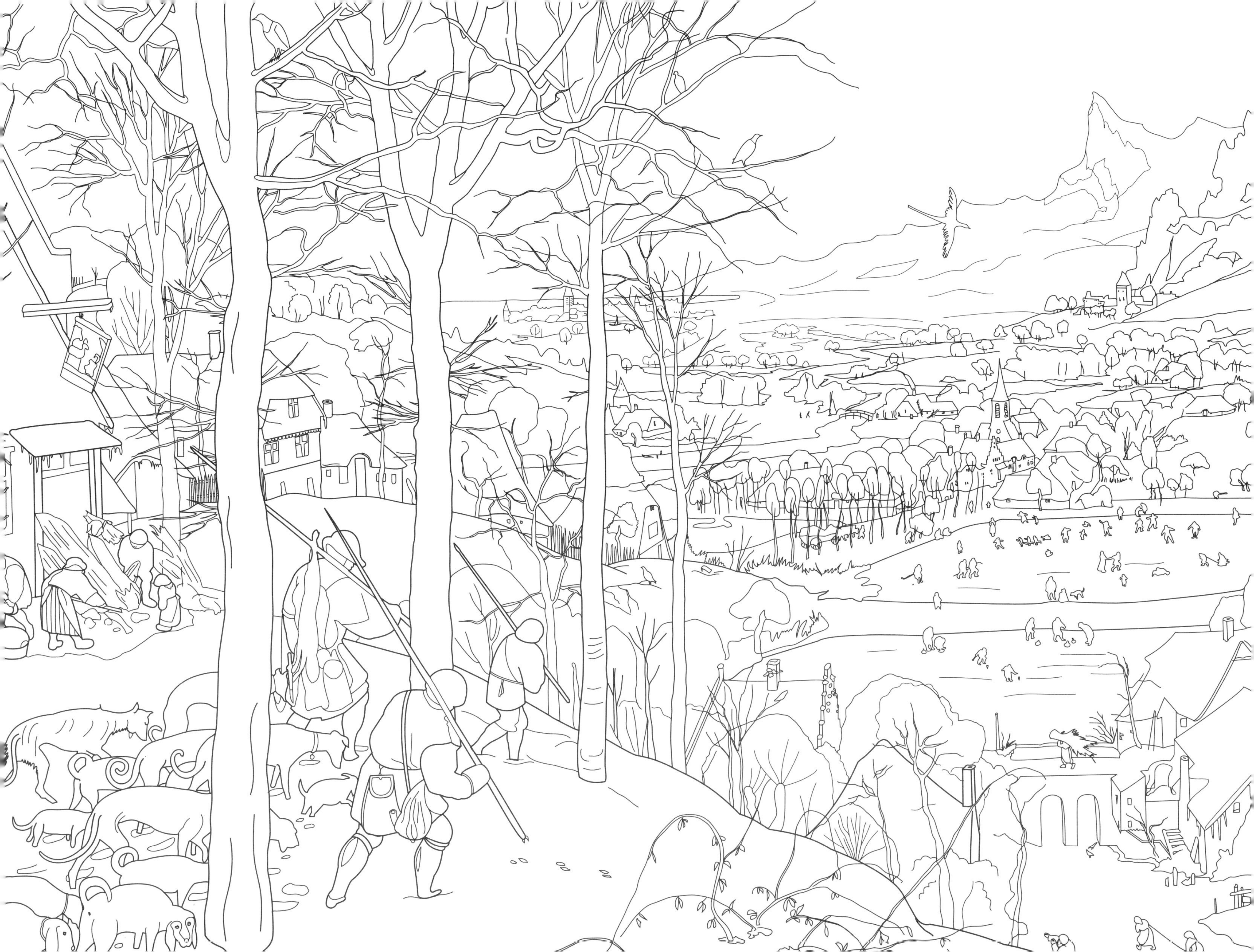

Husain Mirza c. 1586 – 89
Miskina, with Banwali Khord Unknown

The *Akbarnama* (Book of Akbar) is the three-volume official history of the Mughal emperor Akbar, who reigned from 1556 to 1605. It was written in Persian by Abu'l-Fazl, the grand vizier. The illustrations in the book, of which *Husain Mirza* is one, were designed by numerous different artists from Akbar's studio, but the scene shown here is by the court artist Miskina. The details were painted by a miniaturist named Banwali Khord.

This complex painting depicts a battle that occurred in 1573 between Akbar's Mughal forces and the army of Muhammad Husain Mirza, ruler of Kashmir. Both sides in the conflict claimed descent from Timur (Christopher Marlowe's Tamburlaine the Great), and consequently thought that they had a right to rule Hindustan, which Timur had briefly conquered in 1398. The armed confrontation took place in Gujarat, which Akbar had recently left. Muhammad Husain Mirza took the emperor's departure as his cue to invade the region, but Mughal forces returned to drive him out again.

The bustle of the battle scene is heightened by the interlocking human figures. Most of the many colours are flat, but the hatching (closely spaced parallel lines) on the green hills gives the image depth. The intermittent use of gold takes the eye from one section of the painting to another.

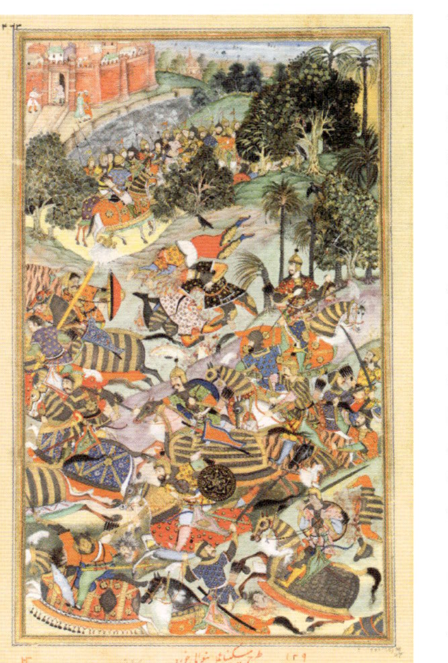

opaque watercolour and gold on paper
38.1 cm × 22.4 cm (folio)
(15 in. × 8¾ in.)
Victoria and Albert Museum, London

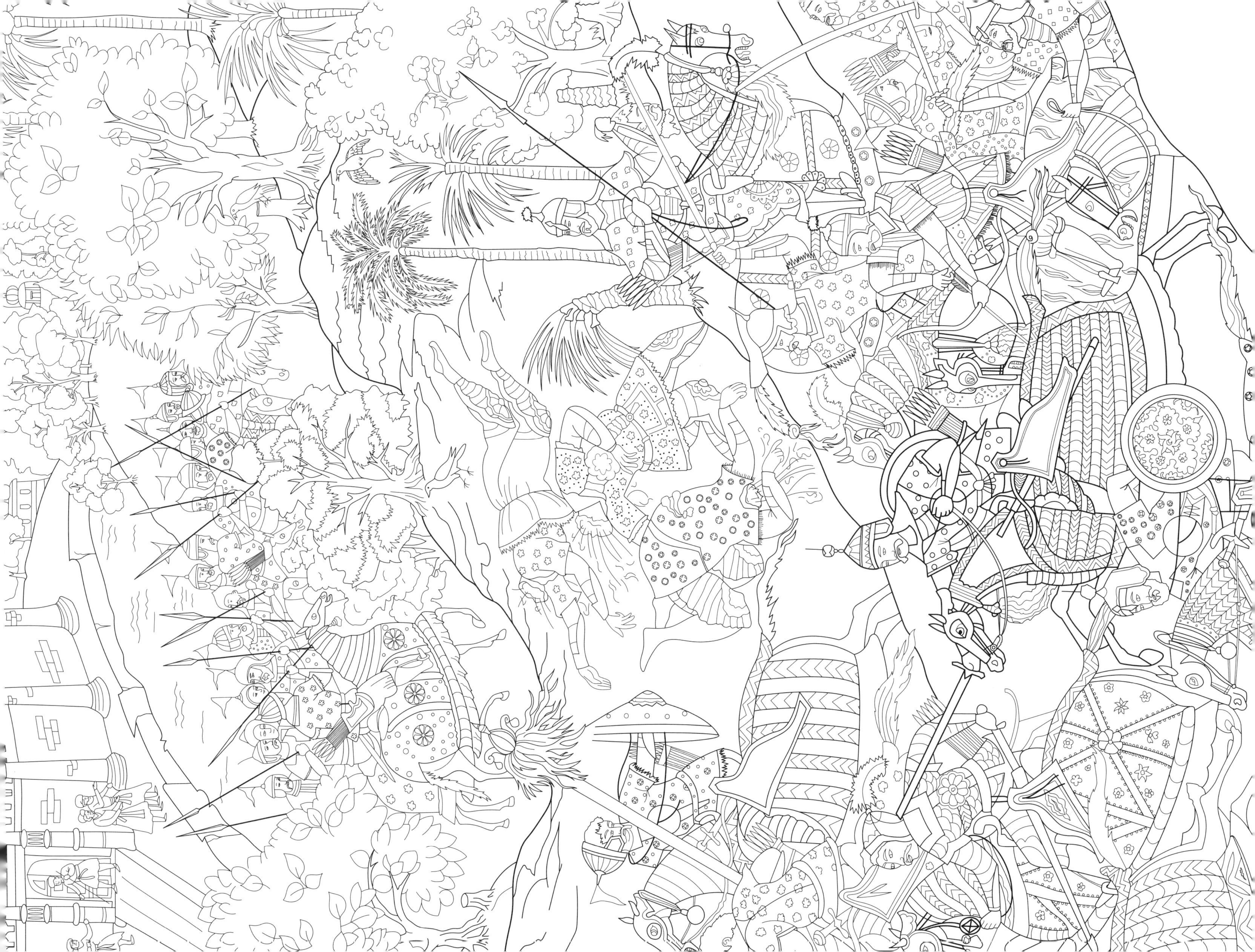

Basket of Fruit *c.* 1596

Caravaggio 1571 – 1610

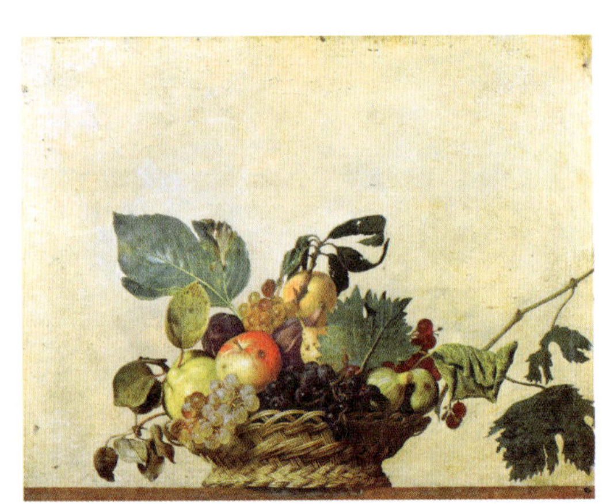

oil on canvas
46 cm × 64.5 cm
(18 in. × 25 ³⁄₈ in.)
Biblioteca Ambrosiana, Milan

Caravaggio (Michelangelo Merisi da Carravaggio) was orphaned at the age of eleven. Soon after, he became an apprentice to the painter Simone Peterzano and rapidly made a reputation for himself in more ways than one. As a painter, he daringly broke the established conventions of his time by depicting people as they really were, rather than in the stylized manner that had been practised previously by well-known artists such as Leonardo da Vinci, Michelangelo and Raphael. Unfortunately, Caravaggio also became notorious for his bad temper, which led to several assault charges before he killed Ranuccio Tomassoni in a dispute over a prostitute in 1606. He spent the rest of his life on the run from justice, but his fugitive status did not stop him painting.

At the top of the wicker basket, perched on a shelf, is a medium-sized peach. Beneath it is a red and yellow apple, with an obvious worm hole, or similar. Also in the painting are an assortment of blemished leaves, a yellowish green pear, four figs of varying degrees of ripeness, a quince and four clusters of red and green grapes. Apart from the quince, all the pieces of fruit and the foliage show clear signs of decay and also damage by moths and insects. It is not known whether this was merely an accurate depiction of the subject matter of the still-life or Caravaggio's treatment of the theme of transience.

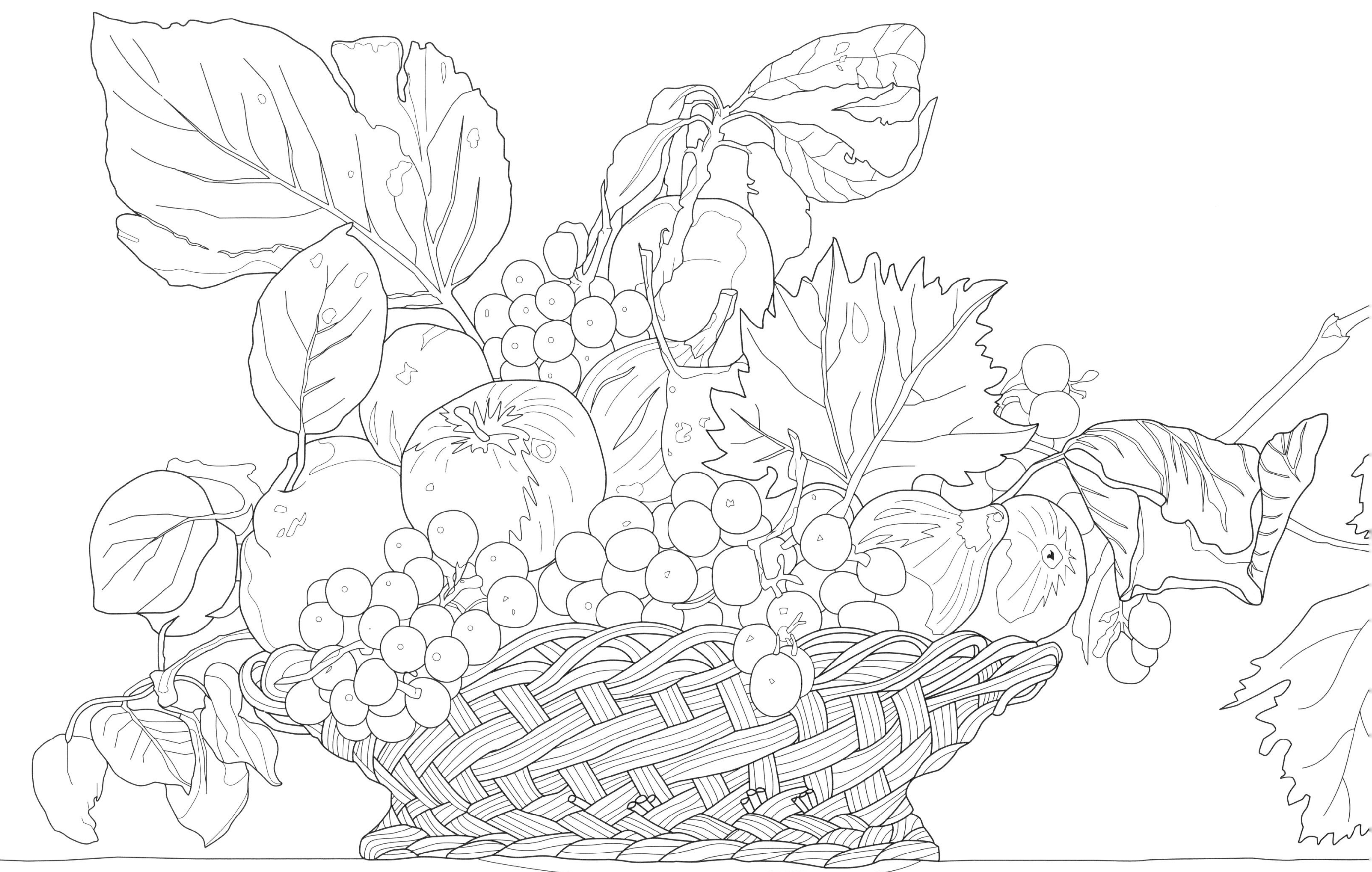

The Night Watch 1642

Rembrandt Harmensz. van Rijn 1606–1669

Arguably, Rembrandt Harmensz. van Rijn was the greatest Dutch painter, but above all he was the unrivalled master of light and shade. He made a lot of money in his youth as a portraitist, but his later life was dogged by personal tragedies and increasing financial hardship.

The Night Watch, originally known as 'The Company of Frans Banning Cocq and Willem van Ruytenburch', is a group portrait of a militia company. Works of this type traditionally depicted their members equally spaced in neat rows or at a banquet, but Rembrandt turned the common subject matter into a dynamic work of art. *The Night Watch* shows the captain of the guard dressed in black with a red sash as he leads his lieutenant, clad in yellow and gold, in rounding up the uniformed ranks. Only eighteen of the thirty-four characters in the scene are portraits; the remaining figures are symbolic, such as the young girl in yellow, who is an allegorical emblem of the guard. The brilliant theatricality of the action-filled painting is reinforced by the dramatic gestures and glances of the members of the guard, and by the various angles of their muskets and banners.

Although the bright reds, yellows and whites in the foreground will not be easy for the colourist to replicate, the real challenge is to capture the essence of Rembrandt's treatment of light and dark without making the background completely flat.

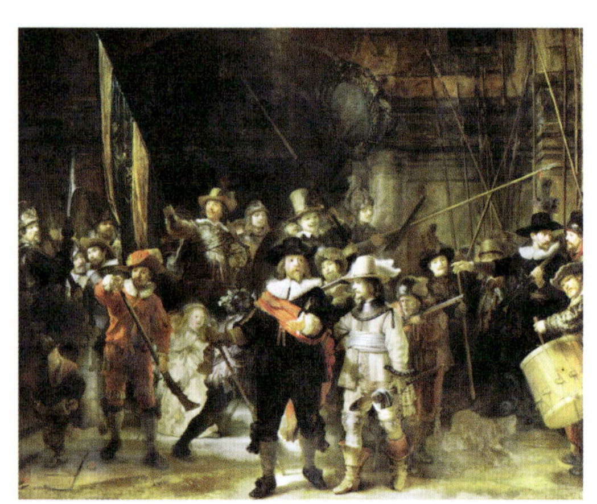

oil on canvas
363 cm × 437 cm
(11 ft 9 in. × 14 ft 4 in.)
Rijksmuseum, Amsterdam

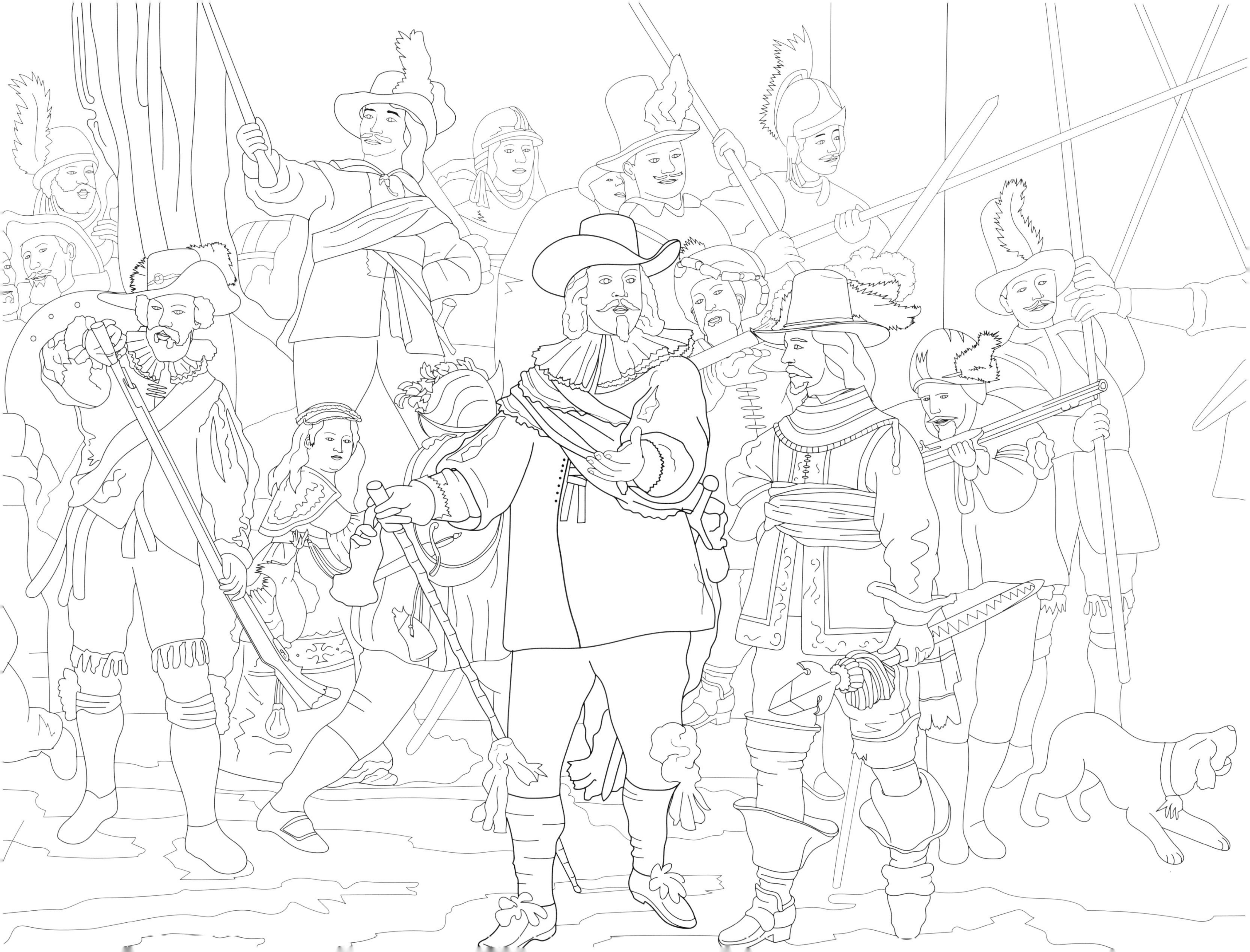

Las Meninas 1656

Diego Velázquez 1599–1660

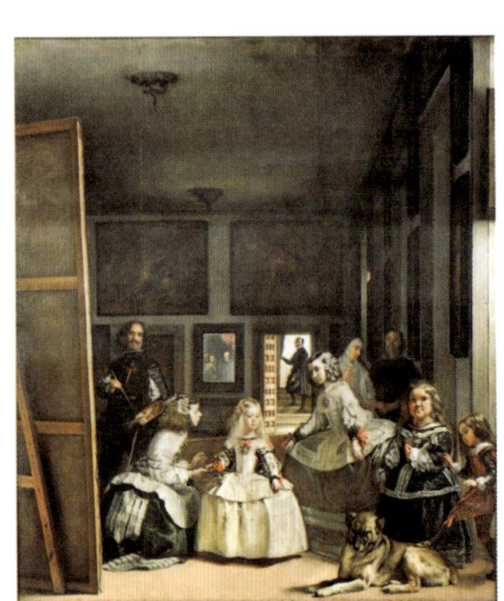

oil on canvas
318 cm × 276 cm
(10 ft 5 in. × 9 ft)
Museo del Prado, Madrid

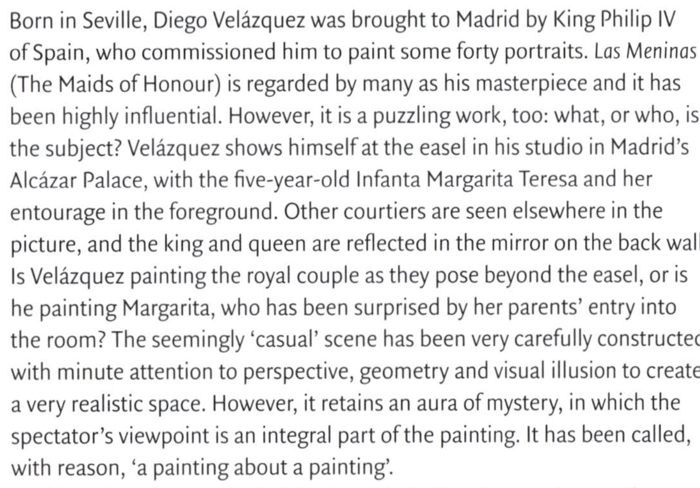

Born in Seville, Diego Velázquez was brought to Madrid by King Philip IV of Spain, who commissioned him to paint some forty portraits. *Las Meninas* (The Maids of Honour) is regarded by many as his masterpiece and it has been highly influential. However, it is a puzzling work, too: what, or who, is the subject? Velázquez shows himself at the easel in his studio in Madrid's Alcázar Palace, with the five-year-old Infanta Margarita Teresa and her entourage in the foreground. Other courtiers are seen elsewhere in the picture, and the king and queen are reflected in the mirror on the back wall. Is Velázquez painting the royal couple as they pose beyond the easel, or is he painting Margarita, who has been surprised by her parents' entry into the room? The seemingly 'casual' scene has been very carefully constructed with minute attention to perspective, geometry and visual illusion to create a very realistic space. However, it retains an aura of mystery, in which the spectator's viewpoint is an integral part of the painting. It has been called, with reason, 'a painting about a painting'.

Using the palette typical of the Spanish Golden Age – ochre, earthy reds and yellows – Velázquez shows how paintings can create all kinds of illusions, while also showcasing his unique fluid brushwork. Although his brushstrokes are a series of daubs when viewed close up, they come together to portray a richly vivid scene as the spectator pulls back.

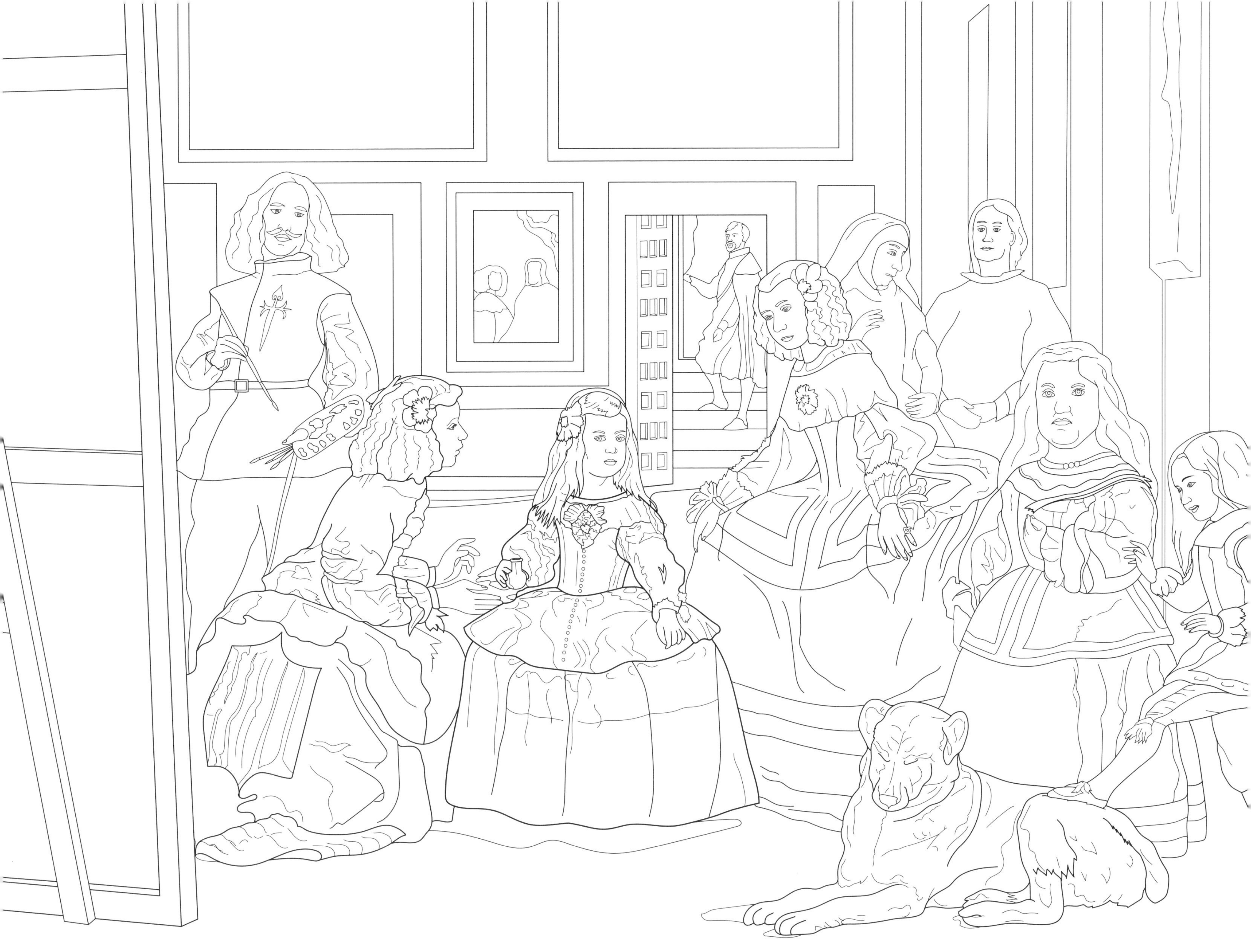

The Art of Painting 1665 – 66
Johannes Vermeer 1632 – 1675

Johannes (or Jan) Vermeer lived most of his life in the Dutch city of Delft. He was not a prolific painter and is believed to have produced only around forty works. After his death, nearly two centuries passed before he received any critical attention. However, when his achievement was re-evaluated by nineteenth-century critics, it became apparent that Vermeer was a great, and previously unacknowledged, master of the effects of light.

This canvas depicts an artist seated in his studio painting a female subject whose eyes are downcast. Light flows in through the window. On the back wall is a map of the seventeen provinces of the Netherlands, flanked by views of Dutch cities. The painting is thought to be a self-portrait of the artist; the woman may be his daughter. It is full of objects that are probably symbolic, such as the plaster mask on the table, but there is no certainty about what they represent.

The patterns of the artist's clothing – black jacket, red hose, white boot hose and black slippers – vary in the light and shadow. The light softens the woman's skin and her blue robes, and it emphasizes the smoothness of the leather-bound folio in her hand. On the chandelier the brass is stronger as it gets closer to the light source, an effect created by applying thick layers of lead-tin yellow, and weaker in the shadows, where the colour darkens to ochre.

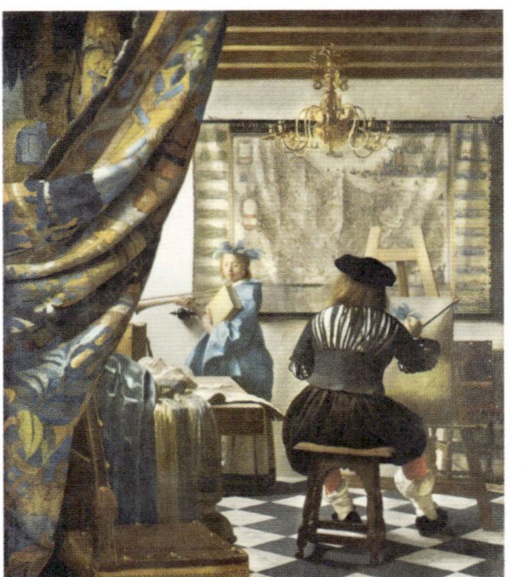

oil on canvas
130 cm × 110 cm
(51 in. × 43³⁄₈ in.)
Kunsthistorisches Museum, Vienna

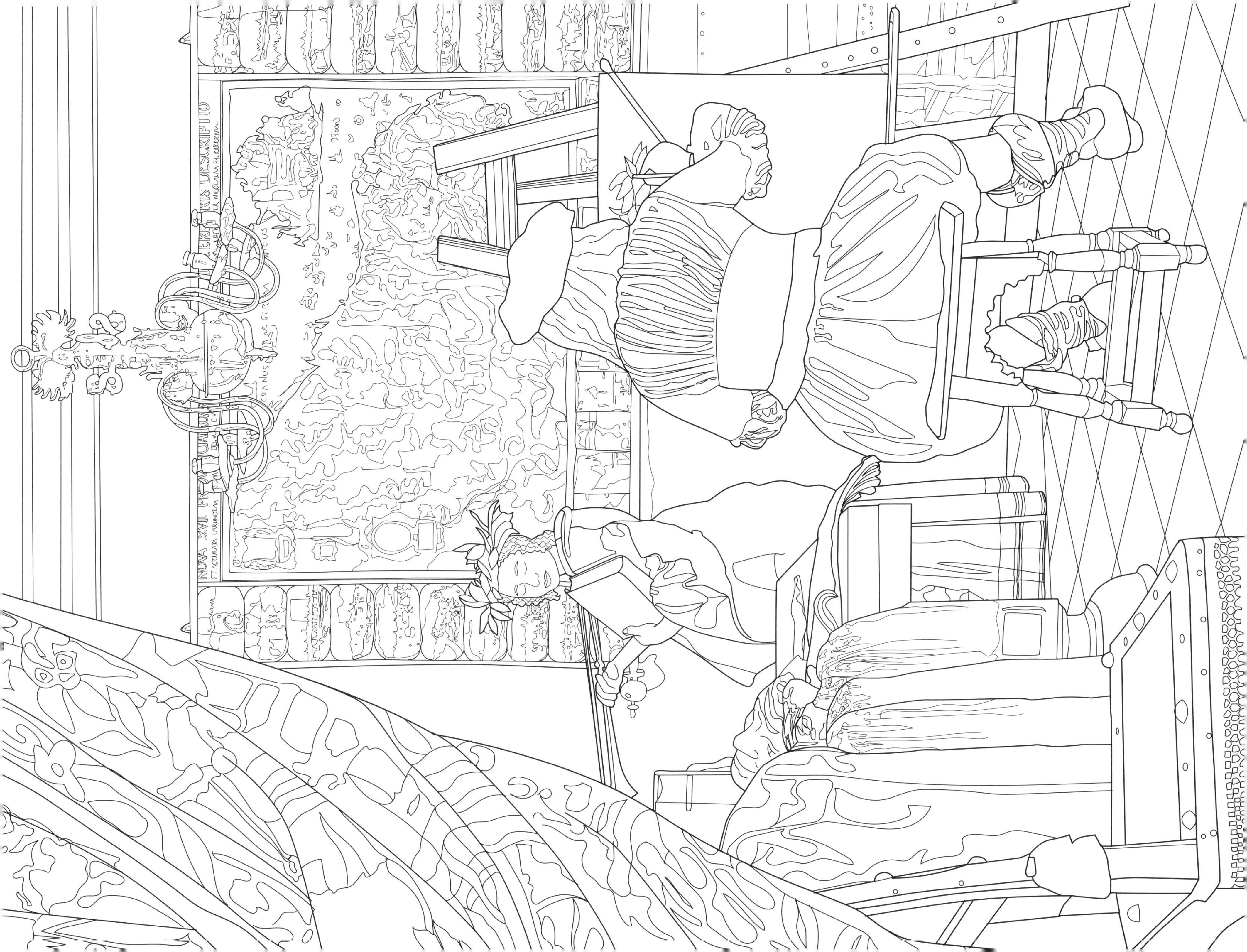

The Entrance to the Grand Canal, Venice c. 1730

Canaletto 1697–1768

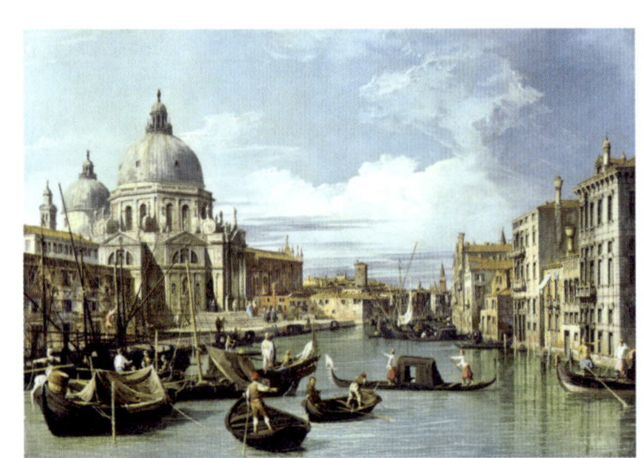

oil on canvas
49.6 cm × 73.6 cm
(19 ½ in. × 29 in.)
Museum of Fine Arts, Houston

Giovanni Antonio Canal – known universally as Canaletto, possibly to distinguish him from his father, Bernardo Canal, a theatrical scene painter – was without equal as a pictorial recorder of Venice. He made a handsome living from foreign visitors who commissioned souvenir landscapes of his native city until 1740, when the outbreak of the War of the Austrian Succession greatly restricted travel across Europe. Tourism dried up, so Canaletto accepted an offer from a patron to move to England, where he produced comparably beautiful landscapes of London.

This work depicts the church at the southern tip of the Grand Canal in Venice that was built to give thanks for the deliverance of the citizens from the plague of 1630. It was designed by Baldassare Longhena in the following year; construction began immediately and it was completed half a century later. Above the octagonal body of the church is a magnificent dome, which is visible from many vantage points in Venice, including St Mark's Square, the bell tower of which can be seen in the background.

From the light on the buildings on the eastern bank of the canal and the shadows on the front of the church, we know that the sun is in the west. The browns of the buildings are enlivened by the bright sky. In the foreground, gondolas, rowing boats and a goods vessel attend a merchant boat that, judging by the clothing of the man on deck, is from the Ottoman Empire.

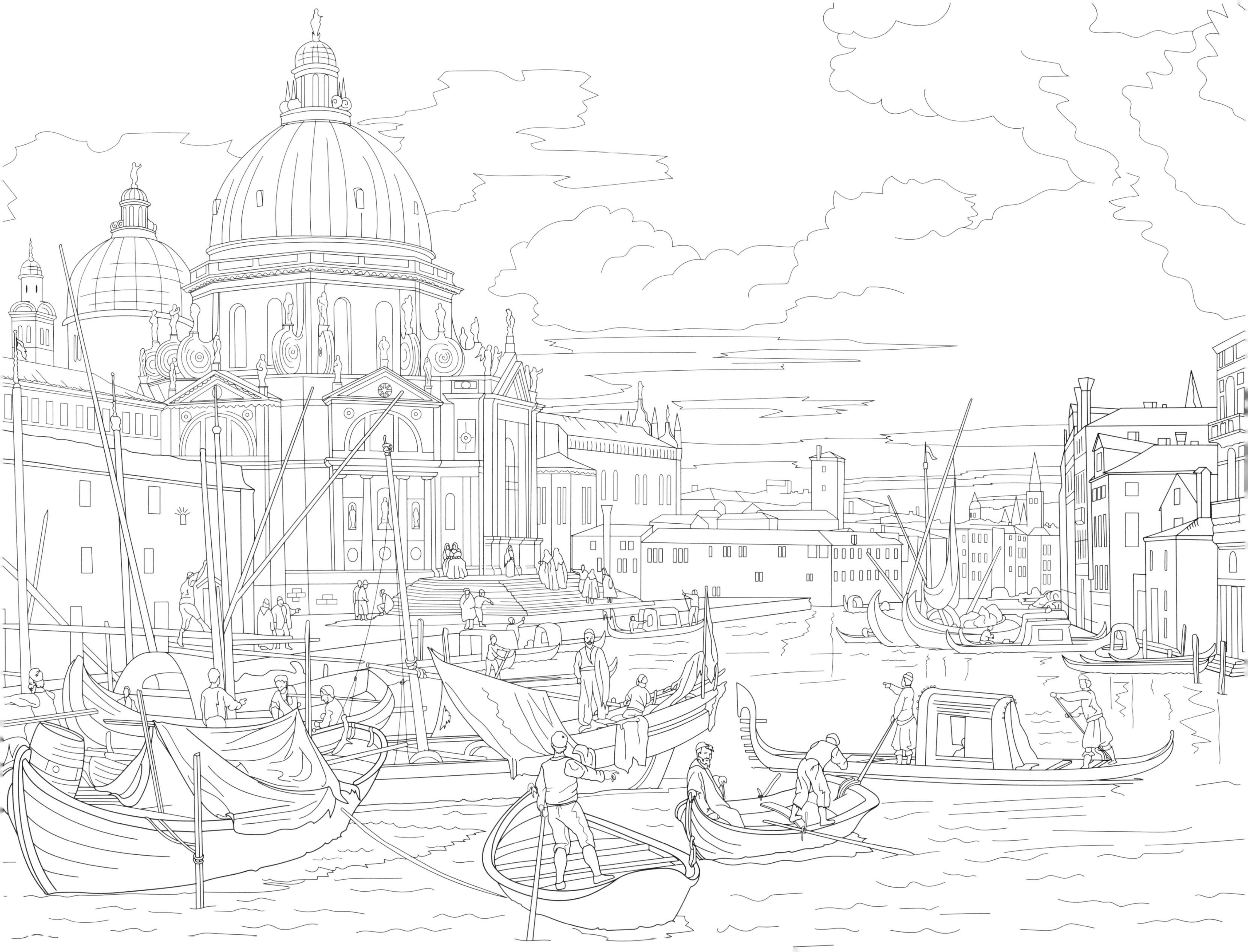

The Swing 1767

Jean-Honoré Fragonard 1732 – 1806

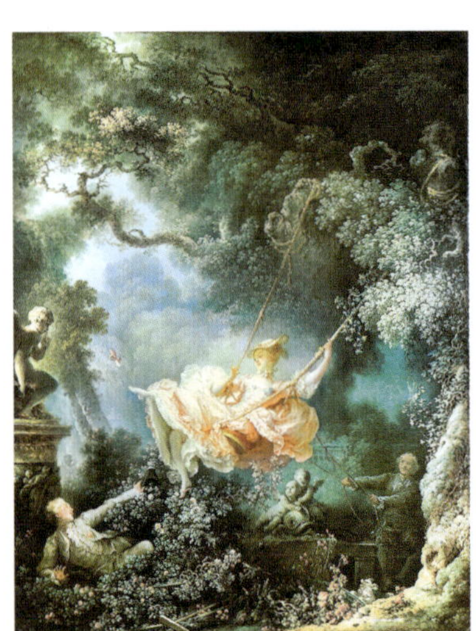

oil on canvas
81 cm × 64.2 cm
(31⅞ in. × 25¼ in.)
Wallace Collection, London

Jean-Honoré Fragonard was the most popular artist in France before the French Revolution (1789 – 1799), but afterwards the frivolity of his work was no longer to the taste of the surviving rich, who were his former patrons. In the new atmosphere of austerity, Fragonard was forgotten; his riches turned to rags and he died in obscurity.

This painting illustrates the elegance and playfulness of the Rococo style. The work was commissioned by an unidentified patron, a young libertine who wanted a portrait of his mistress. In the centre, a swing is being pushed by the woman's cuckolded husband, who is not in a position to see that his wife coquettishly lifts her skirts and flicks off her shoe towards the courtier in the foreground with the outstretched arm. To the left of the canvas, Cupid has his finger over his lips to hint at conspiracy. In the background, two cherubs look on admiringly.

The pastel palette is dominated by creams, peaches and pinks, among various shades of green. Dappled sunshine lights the scene, breaking in through the trees to create a soft, seductive glow. The young woman on the swing (a symbol of inconstancy) is the main focal point, and the highlights are her fair skin and the billows of fabric that swirl around her. However, the rest of the painting is in shadow; the husband, in particular, is in the dark. Although the colours are delicate, the theme is anything but subtle.

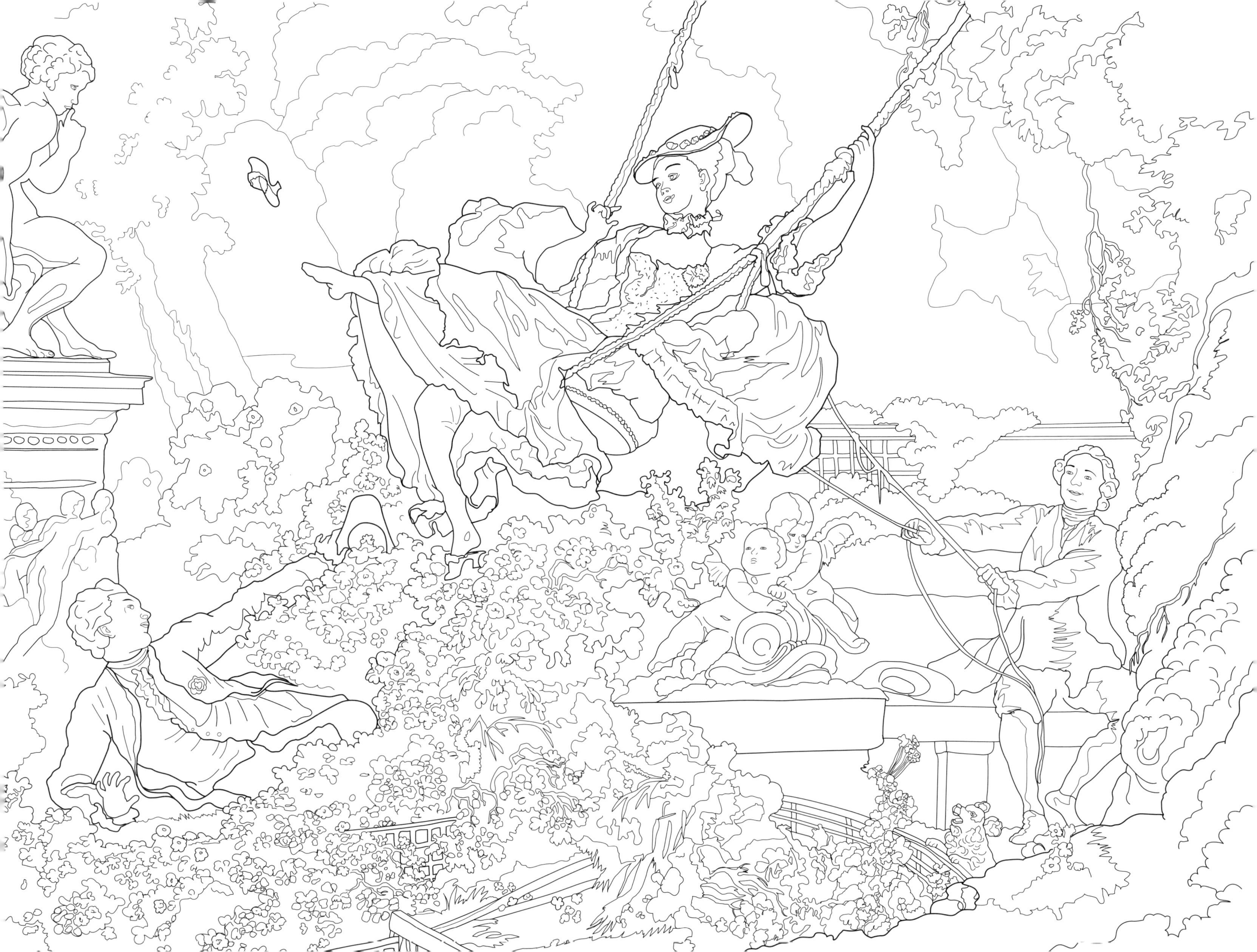

Under the Wave, off Kanagawa *c.* 1831

Katsushika Hokusai 1760–1849

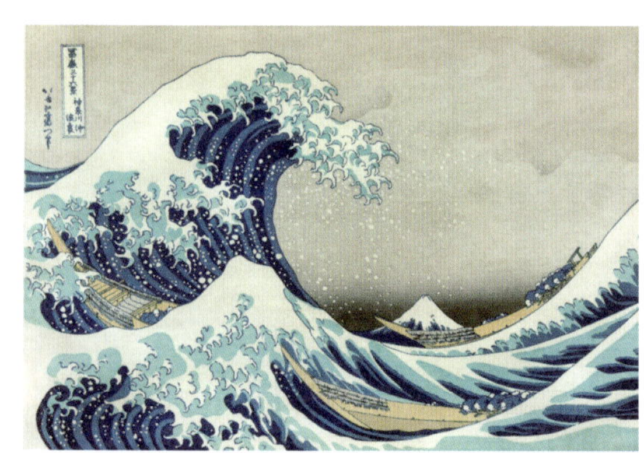

colour woodblock oban print
25.7 cm × 37.8 cm
(10⅛ in. × 14⅞ in.)
British Museum, London

Katsushika Hokusai was a restless spirit, with a prolific and diverse output created under at least thirty different names. He was the consummate master of the long-established *ukiyo-e* school of Japanese art. The term *ukiyo-e* means 'pictures of the floating world', and the work shown here is one of the finest examples of the genre. It is the first in the series titled *Thirty-six Views of Mount Fuji*, for which Hokusai is best known today.

The composition comprises three main elements: the sea whipped up by a raging storm, three manned boats precariously bobbing on the sea and the snow-covered Mount Fuji. In the top left-hand corner are the title of the work and the artist's signature. Mount Fuji is viewed from the east, and the dark colour around the peak suggests that night is disappearing over the distant horizon. The foreground waves are bright because the sun is rising behind the observer: it is soon after dawn. Although the sky is ominous and predominantly grey, covered by what appear to be storm clouds, there is no rain in the picture and the mountain peak is completely clear in the distance.

The great wave that is about to roll over and break frames the composition expertly, but it does not dominate it. Instead, it leads the eye towards the real focal point, the sacred mountain, and on to the fishermen's boats ploughing through the powerful sea.

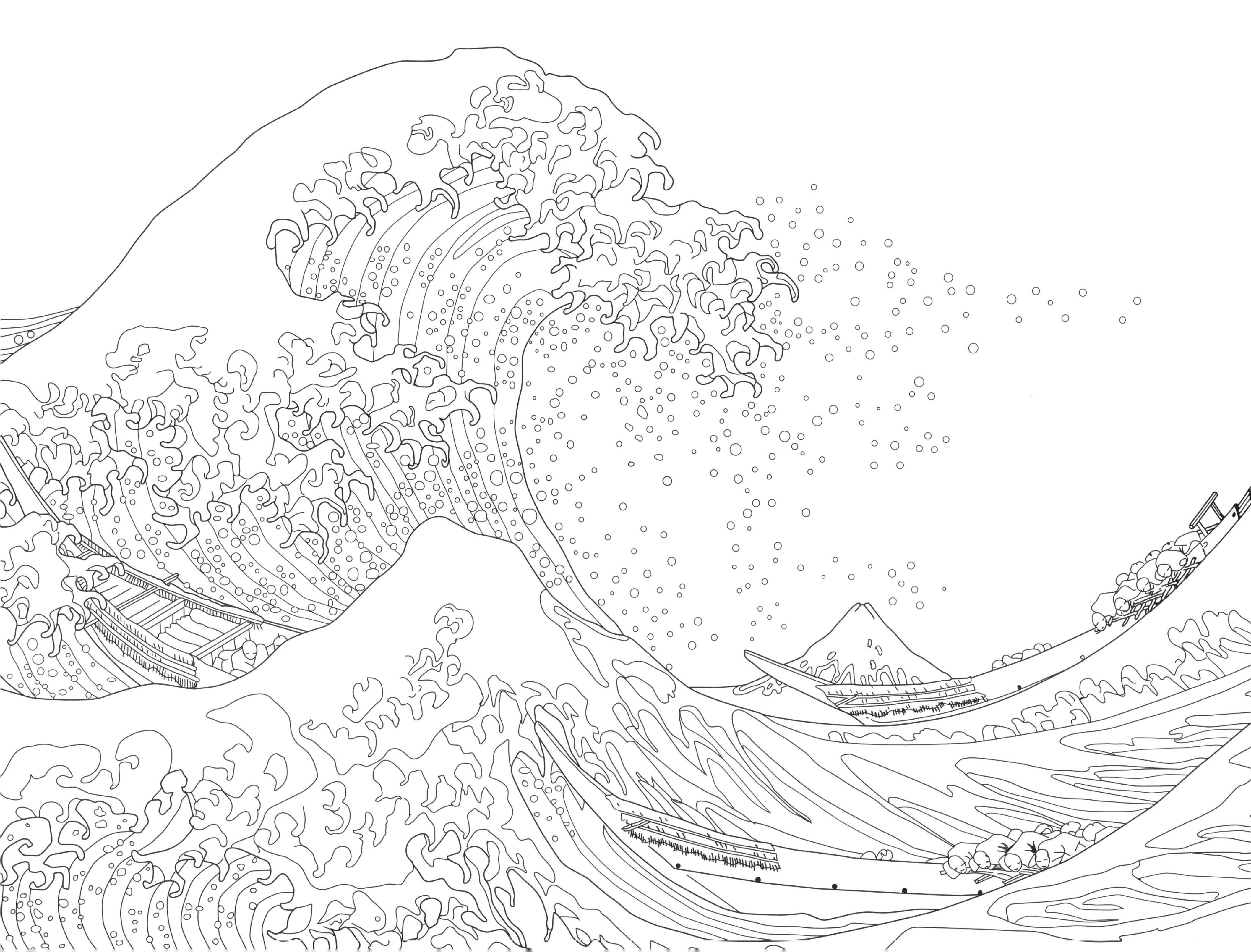

Ophelia 1851–52

John Everett Millais 1829–1896

British painter John Everett Millais was one of the founders, along with poet Dante Gabriel Rossetti and another painter, William Holman Hunt, of the Pre-Raphaelite Brotherhood (PRB). They wanted to break away from established Victorian styles, which they regarded as excessively academic, and return to what they thought of as the emotionally straightforward style of painting that had predominated before the Italian High Renaissance.

Painstaking attention to detail and love of poetic symbolism were characteristic traits of the PRB style. Shakespeare was a favourite source of inspiration. Shown here is a scene from *Hamlet*, in which Ophelia throws herself into a river and drowns after her father has been killed by her lover. Shakespeare emphasized the young woman's plight by describing how she decorated herself with a variety of flowers, each of which had symbolic associations. In the painting, these include crowflowers (yellow buttercups) and white daisies (both of which symbolize innocence), green nettles (to symbolize pain) and long purples (wild orchids, emblems of sexuality). Millais also added red poppies, which symbolize death, and this association is strengthened by the outline of a skull formed by the foliage on the right of the canvas. Every one of the flowers is drawn with an intense botanical accuracy that has been judged by some critics as bordering on the obsessive.

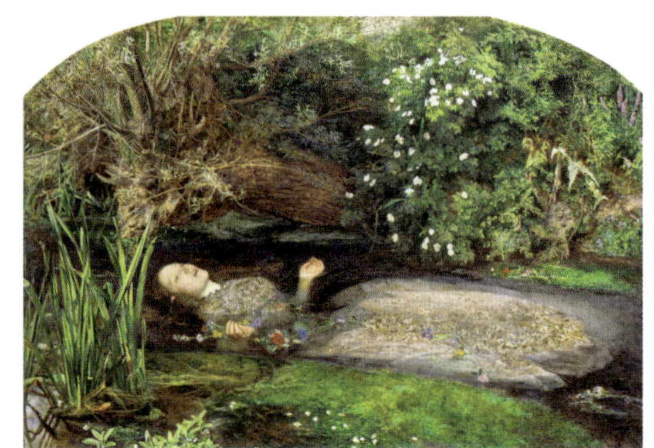

oil on canvas
76.2 cm × 111.8 cm
(30 in. × 44 in.)
Tate Britain, London

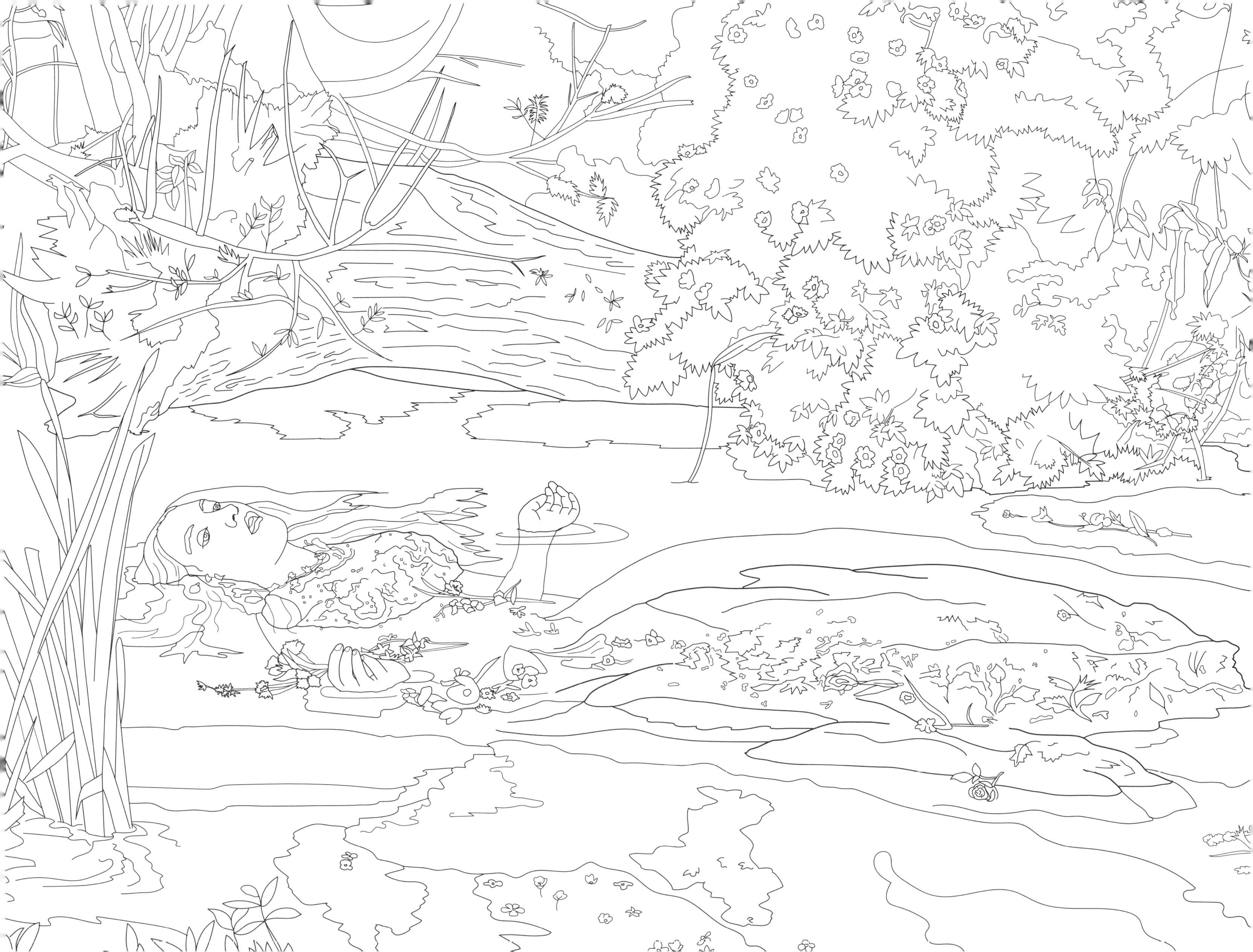

Young Ladies of the Village 1851 – 52
Gustave Courbet 1819 – 1877

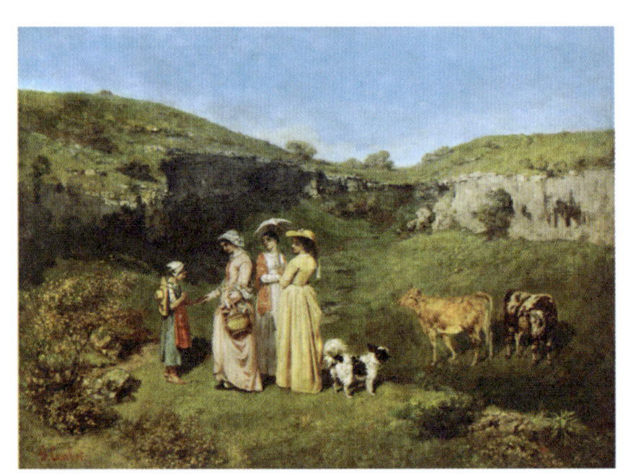

oil on canvas
194.9 cm × 261 cm
(76¾ in. × 102¾ in.)
Metropolitan Museum of Art, New York

Throughout his life, French painter Gustave Courbet was the archetypal rebel. Whenever he saw a convention, he flouted it, in his life as well as in his art. One of his most powerful reactions was against Romanticism, the artistic movement that predominated in his youth. His determination to depict nothing more or less than what he saw before him inspired a resurgence of Realism.

Young Ladies of the Village depicts Courbet's sisters – from left to right, Zélie, Juliette and Zoé. The work was the first in a series devoted to the lives of women. The three girls seen are strolling in the Communal, a shallow valley near their native village of Ornans, in eastern central France, near the border with Switzerland. Zélie is giving alms to a young cowherd.

Courbet seldom, if ever, admitted self-doubt, and widely proclaimed himself to be 'the most arrogant man in France'. He had particularly high hopes for this work, and he was severely disappointed when it was ridiculed. It was criticized for the undistinguished appearance of the models and their countrified costumes, the silliness of the little dog and the cattle, and the absence of traditional perspective and scale.

History has been kinder to this painting, which is now regarded as a masterpiece of artistic truth-telling, especially in its depiction of the authentic summer colours of the French countryside.

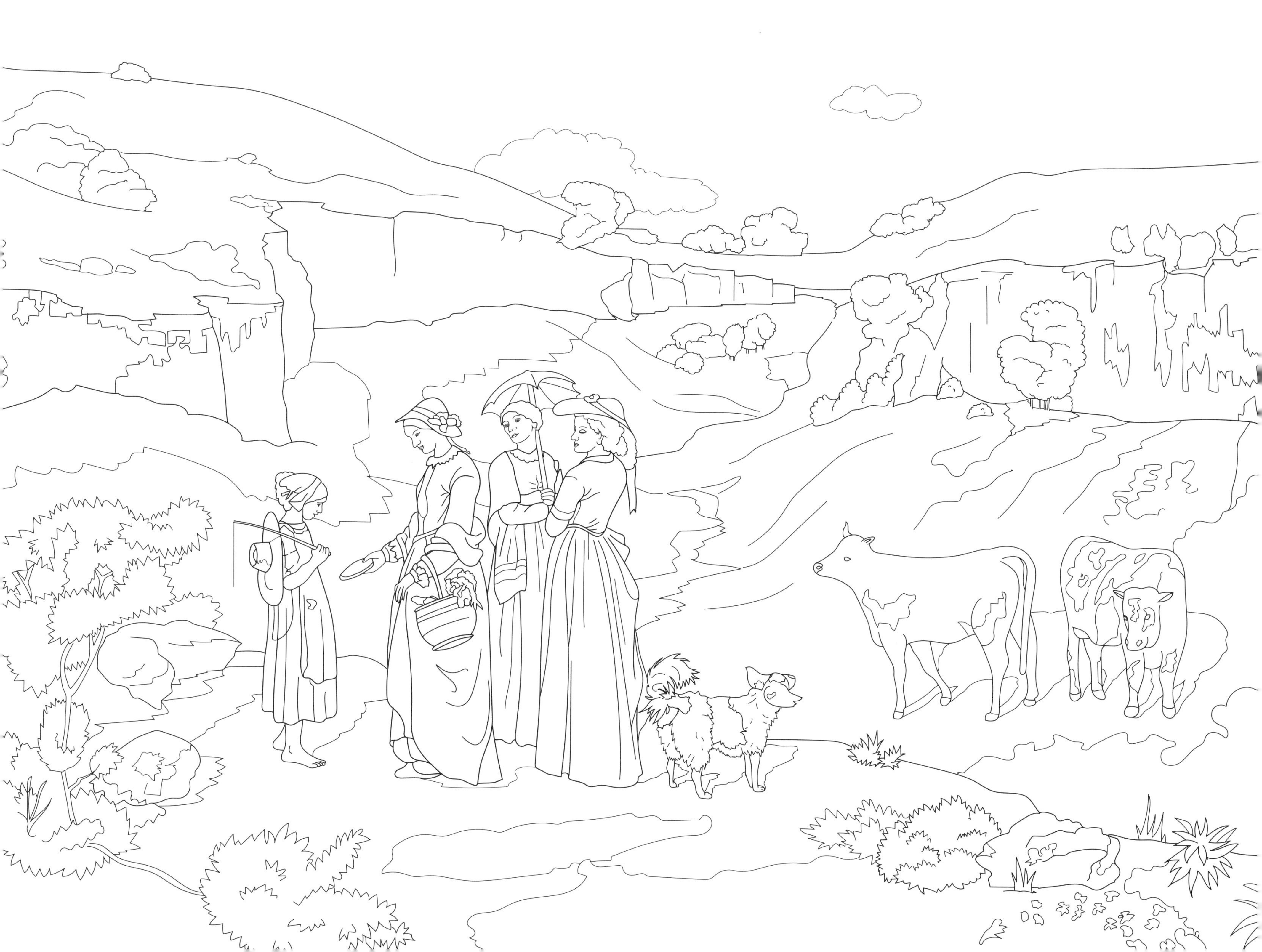

Luncheon on the Grass 1862 – 63
Édouard Manet 1832 – 1883

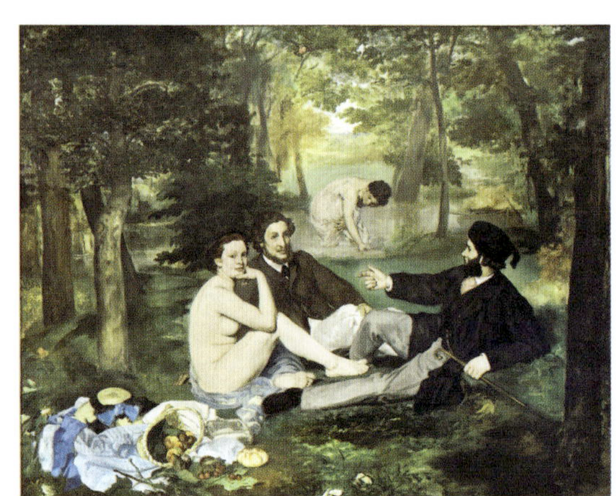

oil on canvas
208 cm × 265.5 cm
(81⅞ in. × 8 ft 8½ in.)
Musée d'Orsay, Paris

As a young boy, Édouard Manet wanted to become a painter, but his parents expected him to study law. He became a sailor as a compromise, but when he displayed no aptitude for seamanship his father relented and allowed him to enter the studio of classical painter Thomas Couture.

Manet was often controversial, and *Luncheon on the Grass* was the first of his paintings to cause a stir in the French art world. Critics acknowledged the artist's talent, but were baffled by his choice of subject. The work is loosely based on *The Pastoral Concert* (*c.* 1510), attributed to Giorgione and later Titian. However, whereas the original is clearly set in an imaginary past, the clothing in Manet's picture is both real and modern. This raises moral questions. Why are two clothed gentlemen sitting beside a naked woman?

Manet's picture is puzzling in other ways, too. The pose of the right-hand figure, for example, is copied from a sixteenth-century engraving by Marcantonio Raimondi. In its original context, the man's gesture makes perfect sense, but here it serves no obvious purpose. The figure in the background is equally disconcerting. She is obviously too large, particularly when compared to the nearby rowing boat. The painting is notable for the absence of shadows and mid-tone colours, and this so-called 'photographic lighting' is deliberately unnatural and inconsistent. Manet was intentionally flouting artistic convention.

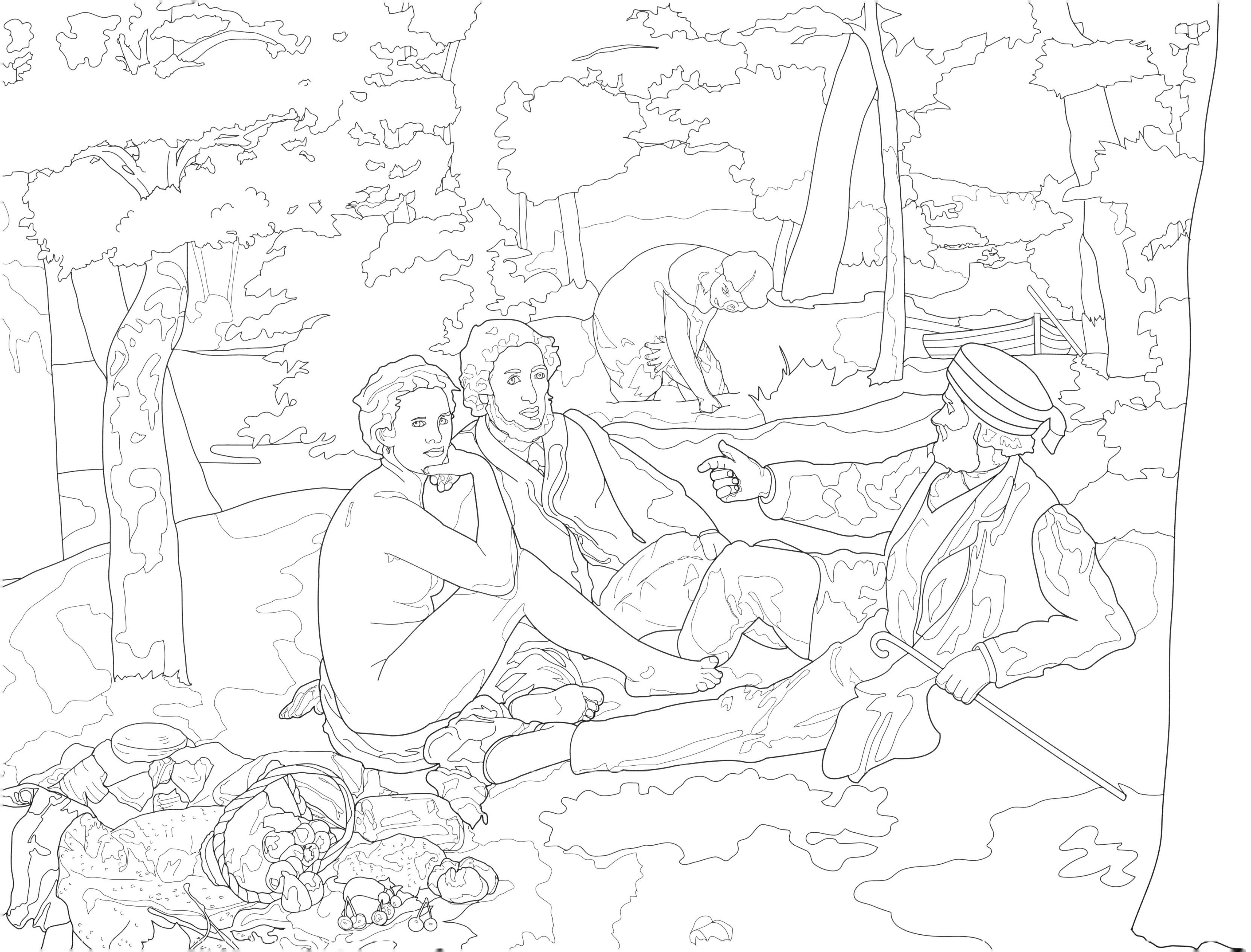

Bathers at La Grenouillère 1869

Claude Monet 1840–1926

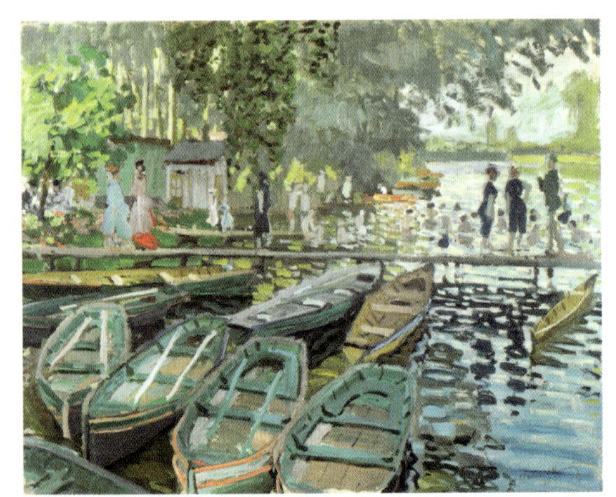

oil on canvas
73 cm × 92 cm
(28 ¾ in. × 36 ¼ in.)
National Gallery, London

The son of a grocer, Claude Monet was born in Paris and brought up on the northern coast of France in Normandy. In the 1860s, he returned to the French capital and befriended other artists, such as Pierre-Auguste Renoir and Alfred Sisley, who shared his interest in the shifting, momentary effects of changing light. It was from one of Monet's works in this style, a painting titled *Impression, Sunrise* (1872), that the group acquired the name by which it is now known – the Impressionists.

Bathers at La Grenouillère depicts a popular spot on the River Seine near Bougival to the west of Paris, where visitors enjoyed the pleasure boats for hire and a floating café. The informality with which the painting has been executed – broad areas of colour for the boats moored in the shadows and white dabs to hint at the party of bathers taking to the waters – suggests that it may have been a preliminary study for a more detailed, larger work in progress at Monet's studio.

Despite this, Monet uses contrasts of dark and light colours to suggest the main flow of the river (gleaming white in the distance), the agitation of the water by the bathers in the centre of the canvas and the ripples around the empty boats in the foreground. The oil paints are daubed and swirled to convey the constantly changing play of light reflected on the surface of the water, which, although calm, is never quite still.

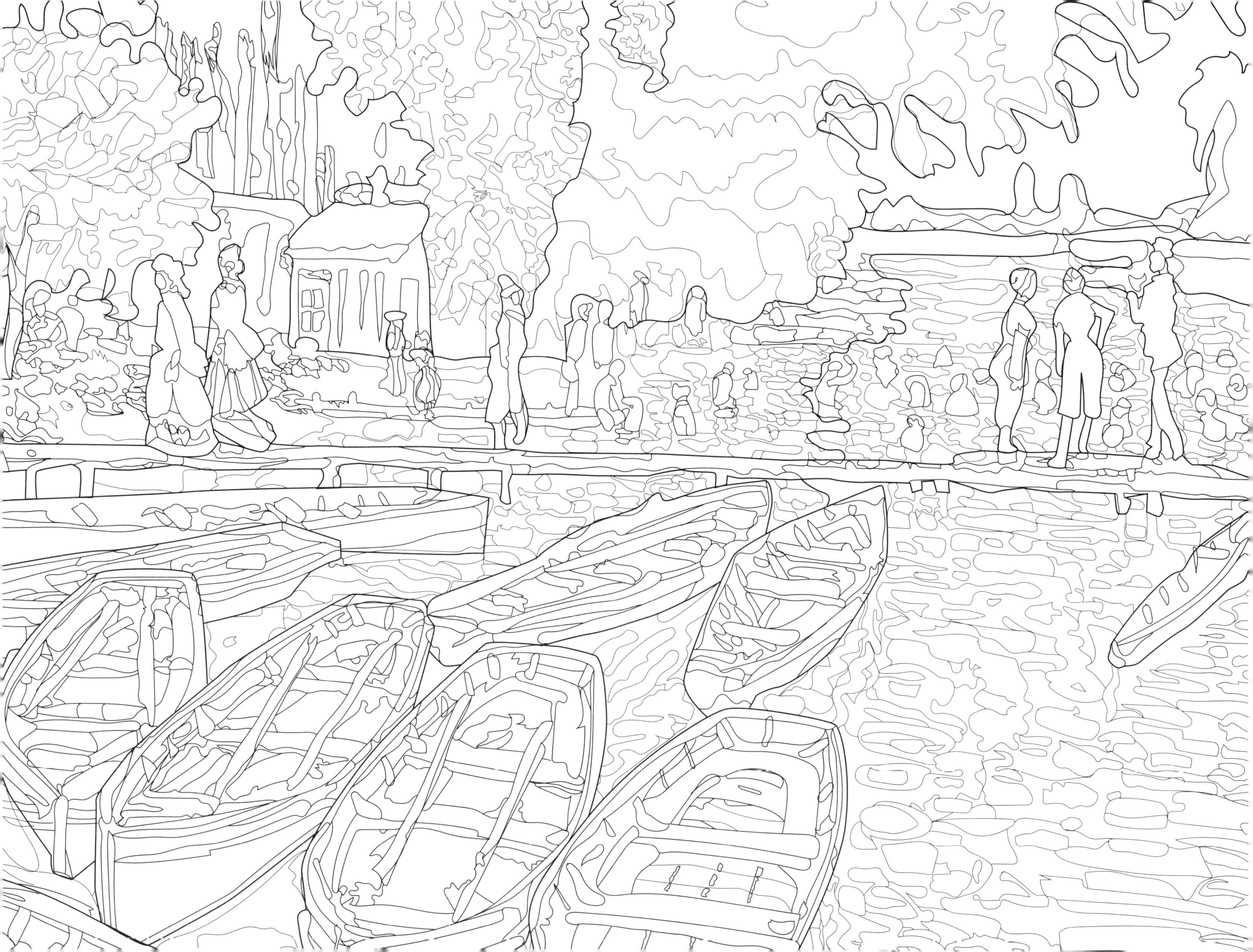

Dance at Le Moulin de la Galette 1876

Pierre-Auguste Renoir 1841–1919

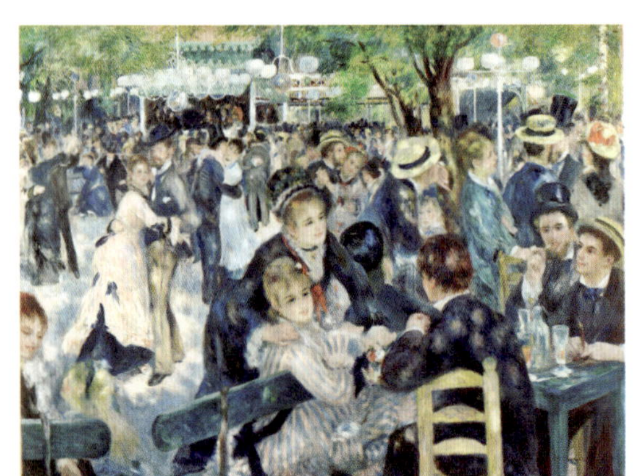

oil on canvas
131 cm × 175 cm
(51½ in. × 69 in.)
Musée d'Orsay, Paris

After an apprenticeship in a porcelain factory in Paris, Pierre-Auguste Renoir attended evening classes in drawing and anatomy at the École des Beaux-Arts, and he had painting lessons at the studio of Swiss Academic painter Charles Gleyre. The latter's style did not appeal to Renoir, who teamed up with fellow students Alfred Sisley, Claude Monet and Frédéric Bazille to form a new approach to visual art that would become known as Impressionism.

This painting, one of Renoir's greatest masterpieces, depicts a Sunday afternoon in Montmartre, a working-class district of Paris where locals would dress up and gather to eat, drink, dance and flirt. Although this work was painted largely in the open air, the people depicted are all either Renoir's friends or models hired for the purpose, so this is strictly a collection of portraits rather than an authentic crowd scene.

It seems to have been painted quickly, in an effort to capture the moment. Renoir creates sunlight and shadow through the use of dappled blues and pinks. Although there are clusters of gas lamps, Renoir's main interest is the light that is filtering through the trees. Note how spots of light from between the branches play on the jacket of the man with his arm over the back of the chair in the foreground. All over the canvas, rich reds, yellows, pinks, purples, blues and greens are highlighted by their proximity to darker tones.

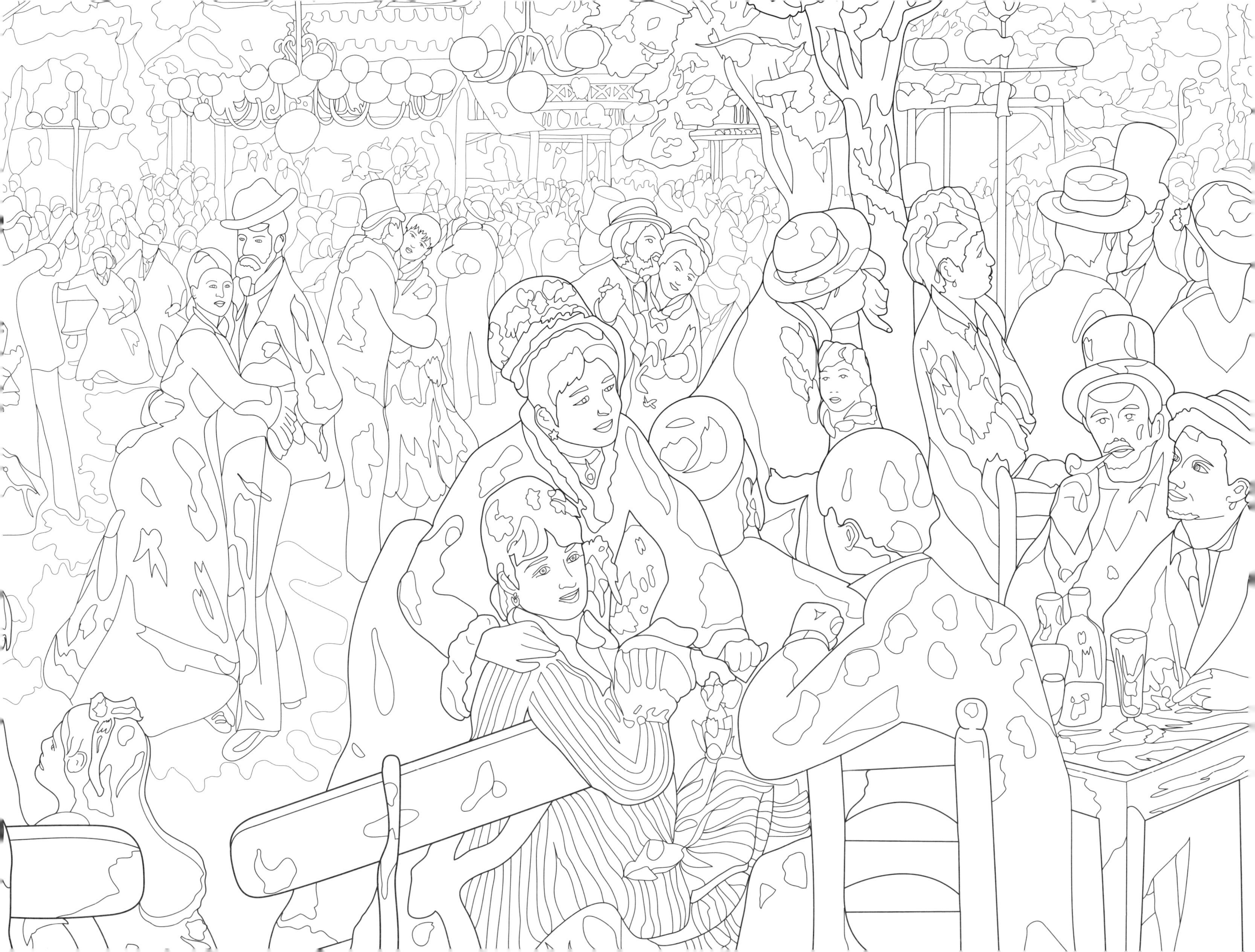

A Sunday on La Grande Jatte 1884 – 86
Georges-Pierre Seurat 1859–1891

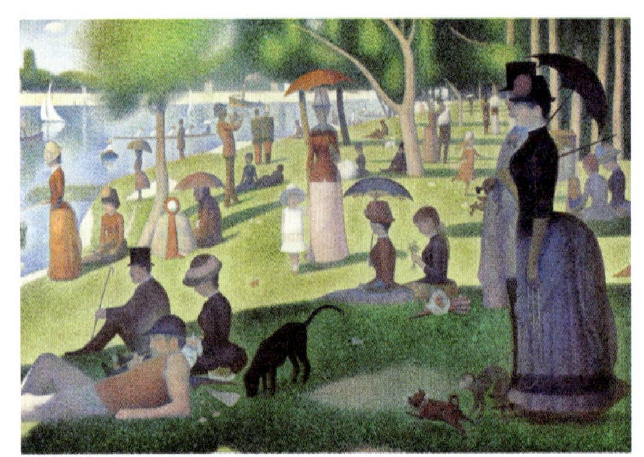

oil on canvas
207.6 cm × 308 cm
(81¾ in. × 10 ft 1 in.)
Art Institute of Chicago

Parisian artist Georges-Pierre Seurat was the inventor of pointillism, a technique that involves the application of colour in small strokes or dots that seem to fuse together when viewed from a distance. Consequently, this painting was not a spontaneous piece of work: the artist made more than seventy preliminary sketches and drawings for this masterpiece. These included crayon drawings of individual figures and oil landscapes.

Seurat took great care in constructing his composition. The contrast between the shaded foreground and the bright background creates a strong sense of depth. There are some disorienting shifts in scale, too, but these are intentional: Seurat aimed to represent modern life in the style of a classical Greek frieze. Overall, the effect is dream-like and haunting.

Most of the forty figures on the canvas are Parisian stereotypes; the monkey in the foreground symbolizes the loose morals of its female owner. The woman with a parasol in the centre of the canvas has a red jacket and an orangey pink skirt. The grass around her is bright green. Both her shadow and that of the running girl in the orange dress are blue. At first glance, the skirt of the woman on the right with a parasol appears purple, but on closer inspection we see that it is comprised of many subtly different hues. A yellow ring separates the hem of her skirt from the surrounding grass.

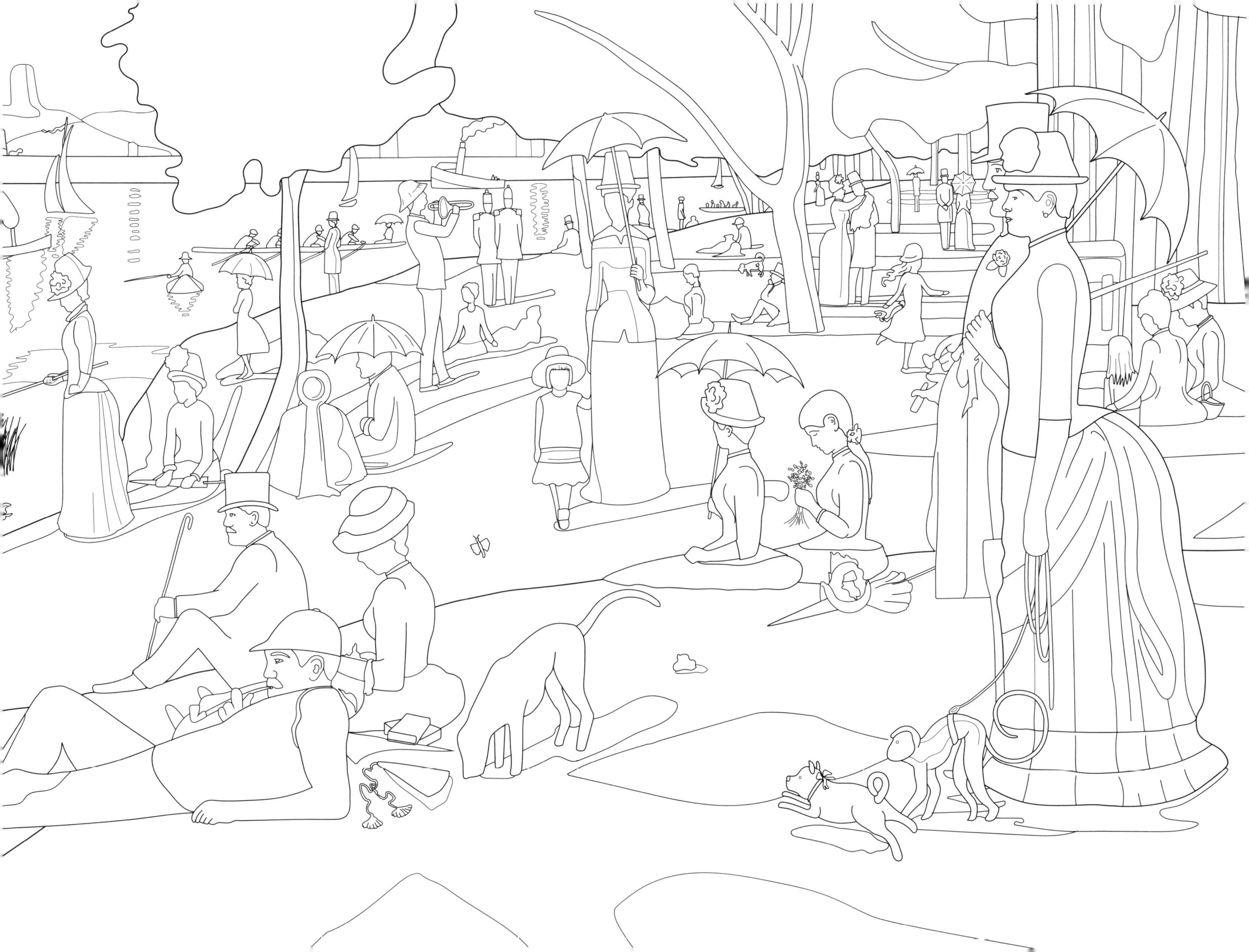

The Starry Night 1889

Vincent van Gogh 1853 – 1890

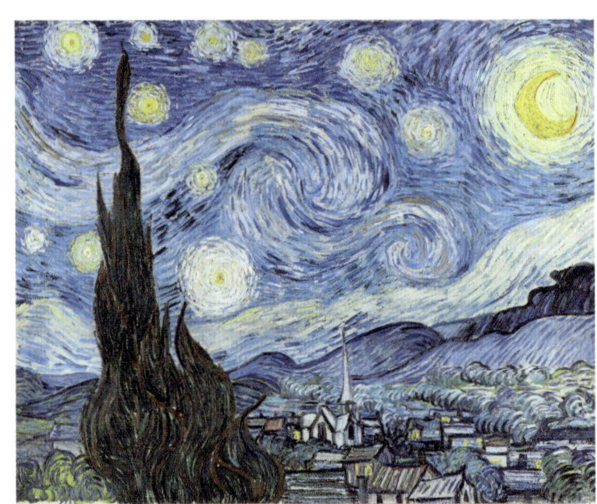

oil on canvas
73.7 cm × 92.1 cm
(29 in. × 36¼ in.)
Museum of Modern Art, New York City

Today, Vincent van Gogh is widely regarded as the greatest Dutch painter after Rembrandt. In his short lifetime, however, he had little success as an artist or in any of his other endeavours. His failures contributed to the mental deterioration that led first to his retreat to an asylum, then to an act of self-mutilation in which he cut off part of his left ear and finally to the self-administered gunshot wound from which he later died.

This celebrated work was inspired by the artist's view from the window of his room in the sanatorium at Saint-Rémy-de-Provence. However, it is not a completely accurate reproduction of the scene before him: the village depicted is an idealized product of the imagination.

Van Gogh painted this same scene over and over – twenty-one times in total – at different times of day and under a whole range of weather conditions: sunny, overcast, windy and rainy. In this view, which depicts the very end of the night, the predominant colours are yellow for the moon and the stars and blue for the night sky. The latter colour is reflected on the hillsides. At first glance, the village buildings may seem shrouded in darkness, but on closer inspection there is the encroaching light of dawn upon them. Historians and biographers have calculated that the depiction of the moon is stylized: at the time Van Gogh made the painting, the moon was in its waxing gibbous phase, not waning crescent as seen here.

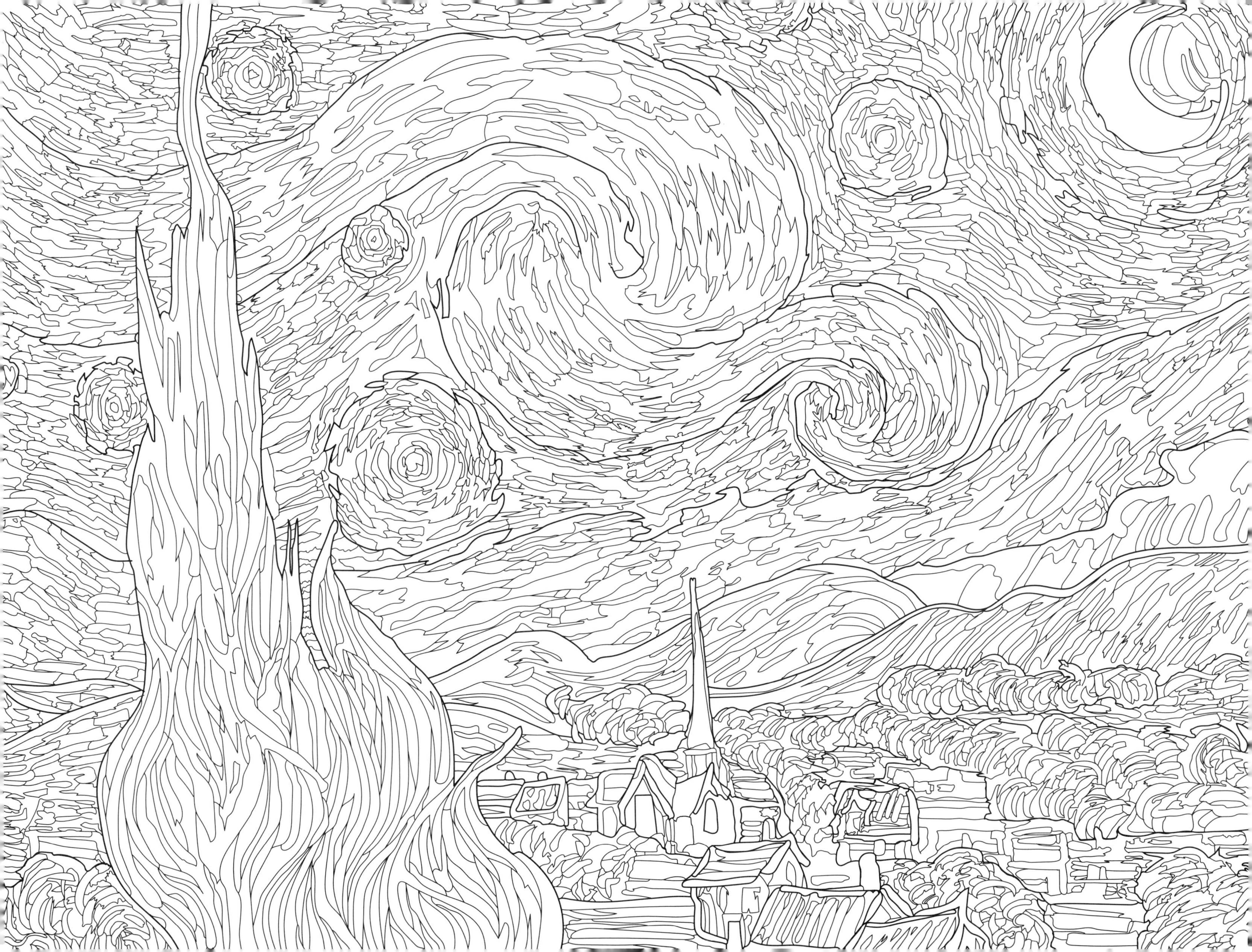

Surprised! 1891

Henri Rousseau 1844 – 1910

The son of a tinsmith, Henri Rousseau left school early and spent four years in the French army before becoming an inspector with the Paris toll office. He began painting seriously in his mid-thirties, exhibited the first products of his labour in his early forties and retired from his day job as he approached the age of fifty to devote himself full-time to his art.

At first, Rousseau's work was a laughing stock: most critics took the view that it was no better than that produced by a child. Gradually, however, came the realization that this was the point: Rousseau was a charming and modest man who produced naive art – but naive is not always the same as simple. This painting – also known as *Tiger in a Tropical Storm* – is a case in point. Initially, it was ridiculed for what critics took to be its infantilism, particularly the somewhat unrealistic depiction of the tiger. Yet there is nothing childish about the slashing rain that falls diagonally from the top left of the canvas. This innovative effect, which lends a three-dimensional quality to the overall work, is achieved by trailing thin strands of silver paint across the canvas.

Rousseau first painted the background, where the greens are deepest, to suggest the depth of the offstage jungle. Approaching the foreground, the predominant colour gradually lightens and eventually blends into a pale yellow in the vegetation closest to the viewer.

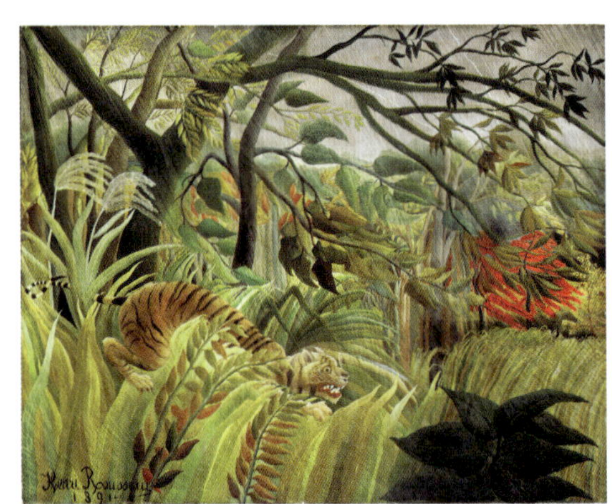

oil on canvas
130 cm × 162 cm
(51⅛ in. × 63¾ in.)
National Gallery, London

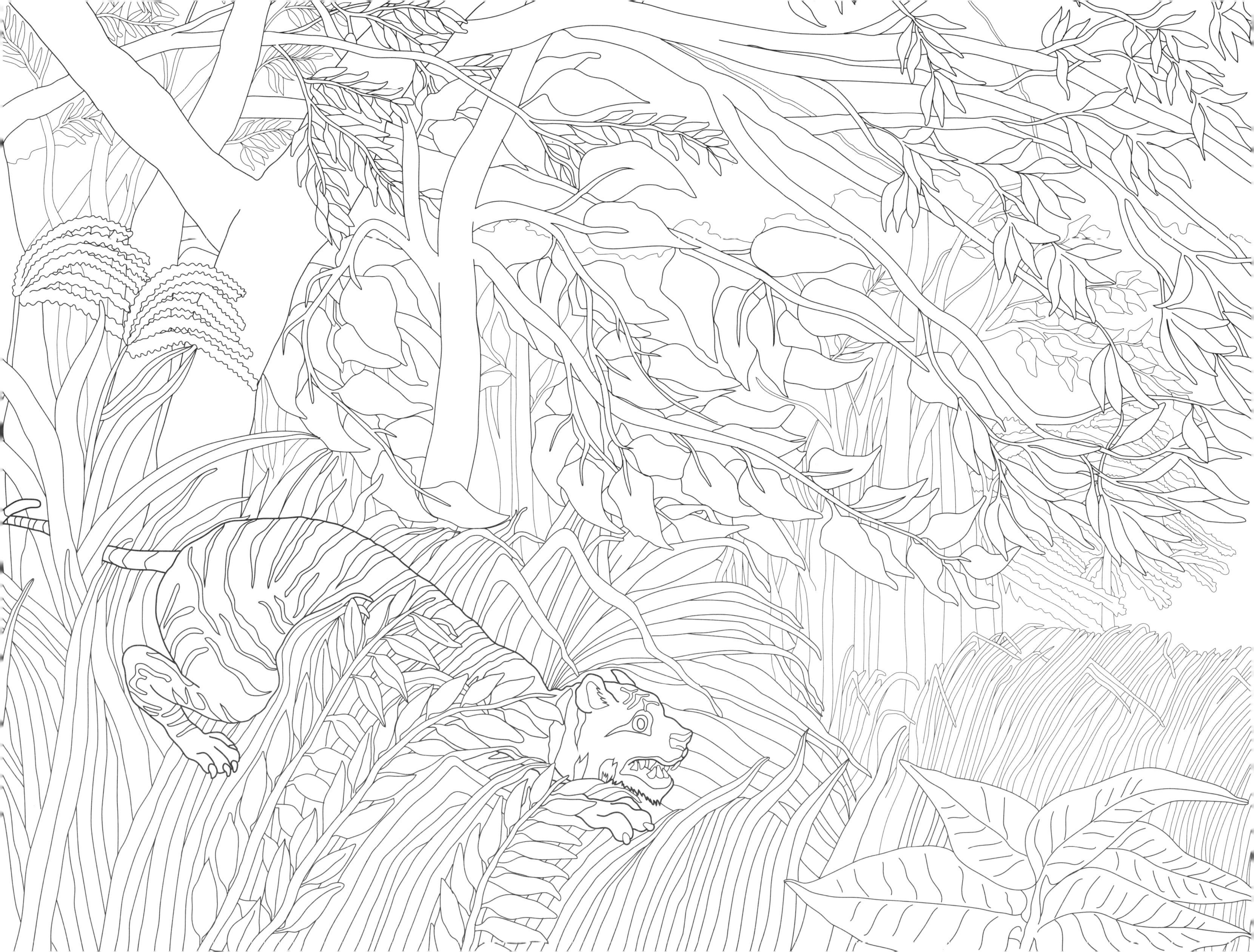

The Scream 1893
Edvard Munch 1863–1944

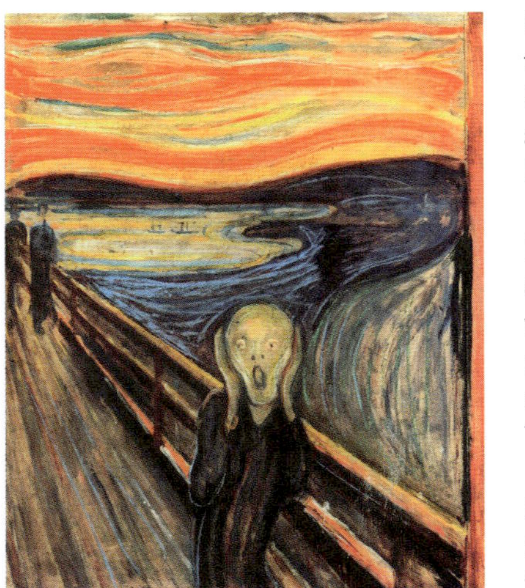

oil, tempera, pastel and crayon on card
91 cm × 73.5 cm
(36 in. × 29 in.)
National Gallery, Oslo

Edvard Munch was a Norwegian artist whose work greatly influenced the style later known as German Expressionism. He grew up in Kristiania (now Oslo) and then worked in Paris and Berlin. He was a friend of two great compatriot contemporaries: playwright Henrik Ibsen and classical composer Edvard Grieg.

The Scream is one of the most familiar images in world art. It was inspired by a panic attack that the artist suffered while strolling along a path outside Kristiania. As he later described the event: 'The sun was setting and the clouds turned as red as blood. I sensed a scream passing through nature. I felt as though I could actually hear the scream. I painted this picture, painted the clouds like real blood. The colours shrieked.'

Munch represents the 'scream' through a series of undulating lines that press in on the central figure like shock waves, reducing its face to a primal image of fear. He accentuates the effect of his frenzied brushwork by showing that the two people in the background remain unscathed, thus implying that the trauma comes from the figure's own mind, rather than the world outside. Viewers have little difficulty understanding the horror, pain and anguish being expressed in this work. On a copy of the picture, Munch wrote: 'Could only have been painted by a madman.'

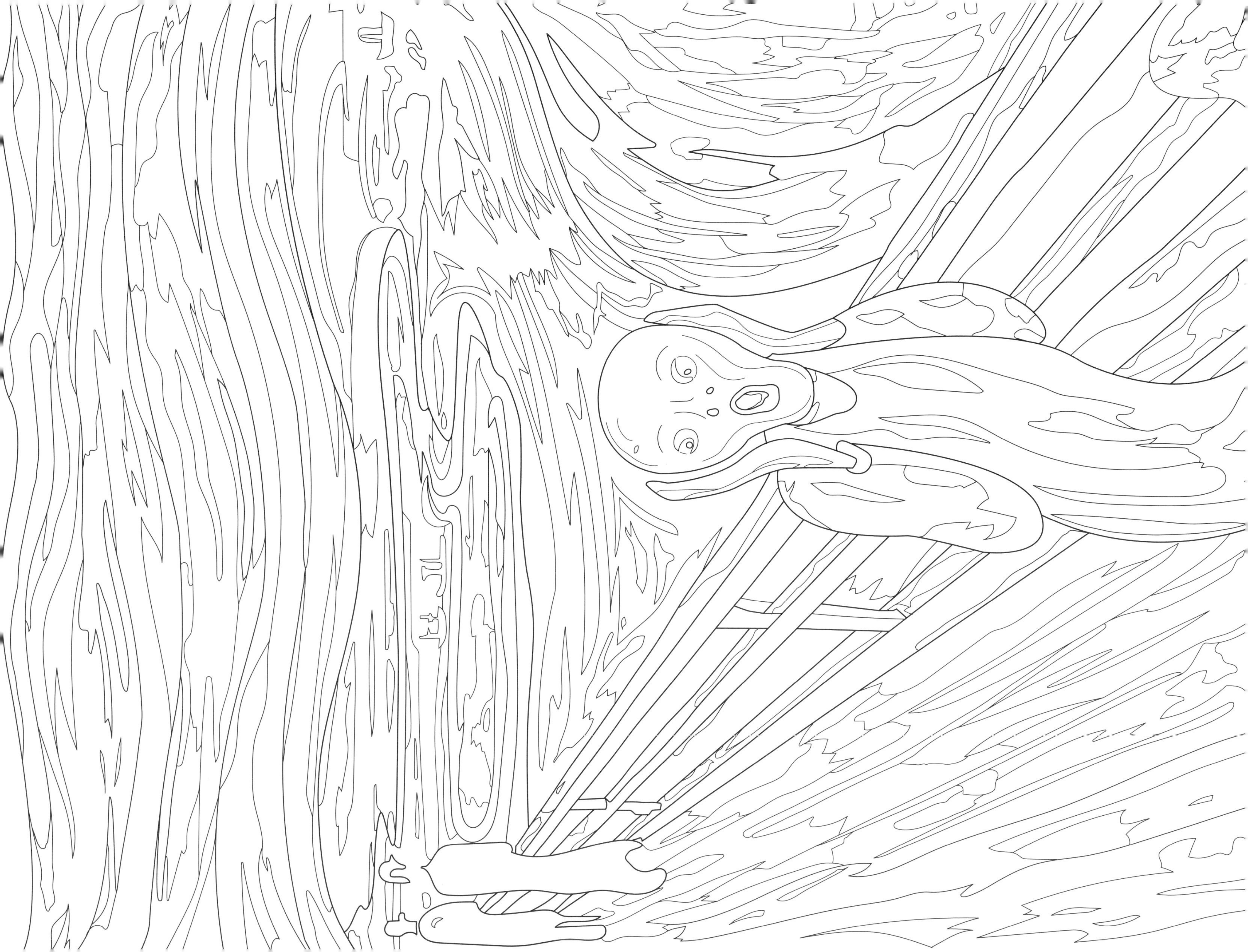

Bathers *c. 1894 – 1905*
Paul Cézanne 1839 – 1906

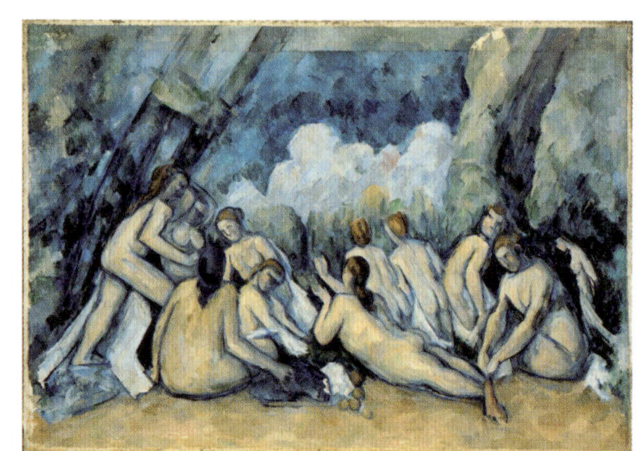

oil on canvas
127.2 cm × 196.1 cm
(50 in. × 77 ¼ in.)
National Gallery, London

Paul Cézanne is widely regarded as the father of twentieth-century painting, but success came to him late in life. Although he took part in the first exhibition of Impressionist paintings in 1874, he soon lost interest in painting the effects of light and became increasingly preoccupied with shape, mass and colour. He abandoned traditional graphical representations of perspective and developed a more abstract method of creating three-dimensionality through the application of patches of different colours. Although Cézanne painted from nature, he would distort at will if he believed that this suited his artistic purpose.

This painting – also known as *Les Grandes Baigneuses* – was one of a series in which the artist strove to convey a sense of eroticism, not so much through the depiction of nude figures as through the sensuous liquidity of the paint and the oiliness of the pigment. Observe how the shapes of the women are accurate geometrically but their faces are little more than rudimentary. All the colours are pure and flat, and the earthy skin tones of the human figures interact dynamically with the greens, blues and yellows of the background scene.

There is no obvious narrative to the painting, although the woman on the far left seems to be arriving and some of the figures in the centre of the canvas may be preparing to leave.

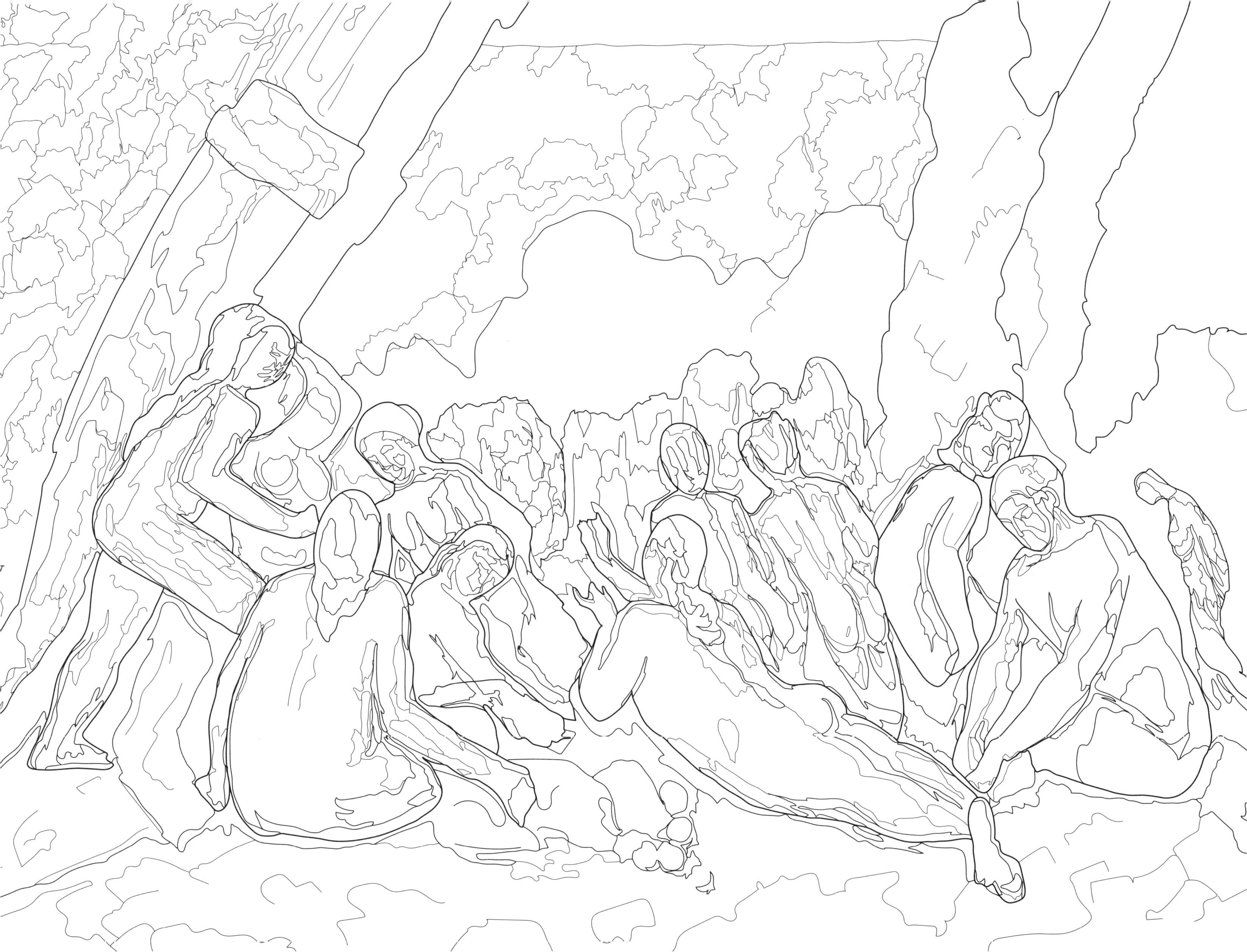

Nevermore 1897

Paul Gauguin 1848–1903

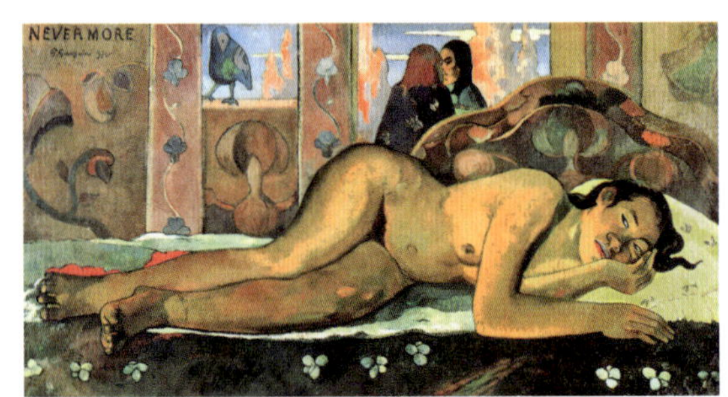

oil on canvas
50 cm × 116 cm
(19 ⅝ in. × 45 ⅝ in.)
Courtauld Gallery, London

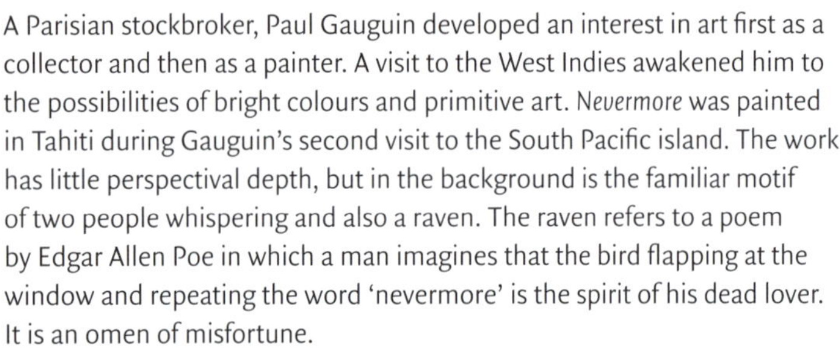

A Parisian stockbroker, Paul Gauguin developed an interest in art first as a collector and then as a painter. A visit to the West Indies awakened him to the possibilities of bright colours and primitive art. *Nevermore* was painted in Tahiti during Gauguin's second visit to the South Pacific island. The work has little perspectival depth, but in the background is the familiar motif of two people whispering and also a raven. The raven refers to a poem by Edgar Allen Poe in which a man imagines that the bird flapping at the window and repeating the word 'nevermore' is the spirit of his dead lover. It is an omen of misfortune.

The naked girl reclines facing the viewer, but her body is not erotic in the tradition of Western painting. The curve of her hip is exaggerated to mimic that of the headboard behind her, and both lines are accentuated by the strong verticals in the background. She remains watchful as she listens to the whisperers, and the raven, in turn, watches her.

The broad areas of flat colour have dark outlines, which emphasize that the canvas is more decorative than representational. Gauguin's use of colour is unconventional: the raven is not black, as might be expected, but a bright, gaudy mix of blue and green. Note, too, how the broad, narrow painting is united by the flash of red on the lips of the reclining woman and the reappearance of the same colour in the fabric at her feet.

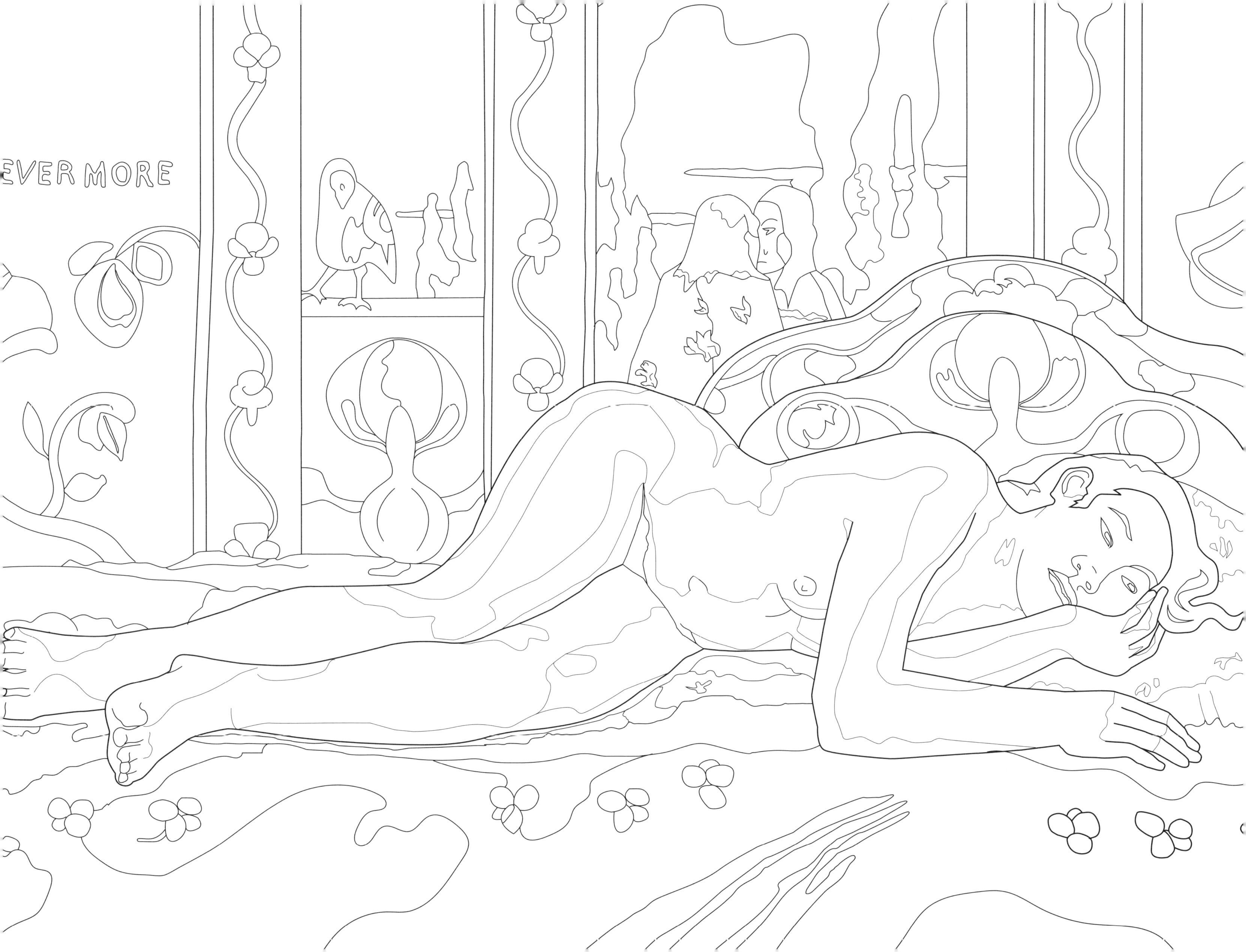
EVER MORE

The Kiss 1908–09
Gustav Klimt 1862–1918

Austrian artist Gustav Klimt painted murals in traditional Academic style until he revolted against classicism and co-founded the Vienna Secession in 1897, which was not so much an identifiable style as a protest against conformity. *The Kiss* epitomizes this movement.

The huge painting is a riotous depiction of sexual love, in which Klimt incorporates numerous styles from almost any time and place other than his own: the spiral patterns of the woman's dress are derived from Bronze Age art; the simple composition and the location of the man's head at the very top of the canvas recall Japanese prints; the geometric patterning is Art Nouveau and the juxtaposition of two- and three-dimensional figures reflects the influence of Paul Cézanne and Edgar Degas.

Most dominant in the image is the golden shroud, from which the representational forms emerge only gradually. The background may be taken to suggest a night sky, and the predominantly green but multicoloured foreground a flowery meadow. There is a womb-like security here, but there is also potential danger: the lovers look as if they might fall to Earth or be enveloped by the darkness. The woman's head is contorted, her toes are bent and the colouration of her flesh suggests putrefaction. *The Kiss* celebrates sex, but does not over-romanticize it.

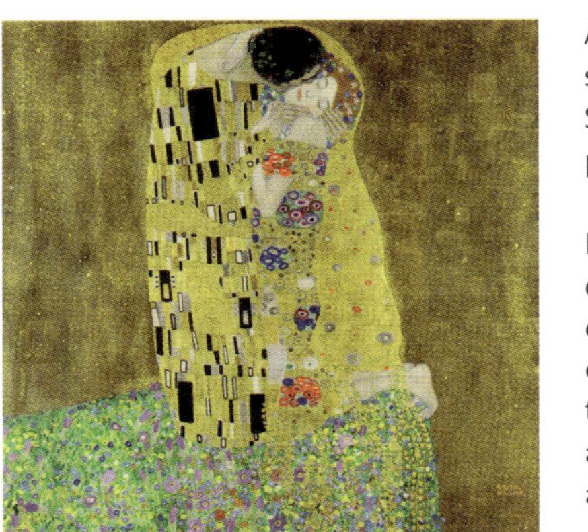

oil, gold and silver leaf on canvas
180 cm × 180 cm
(70⅞ in. × 70⅞ in.)
Belvedere Palace, Vienna

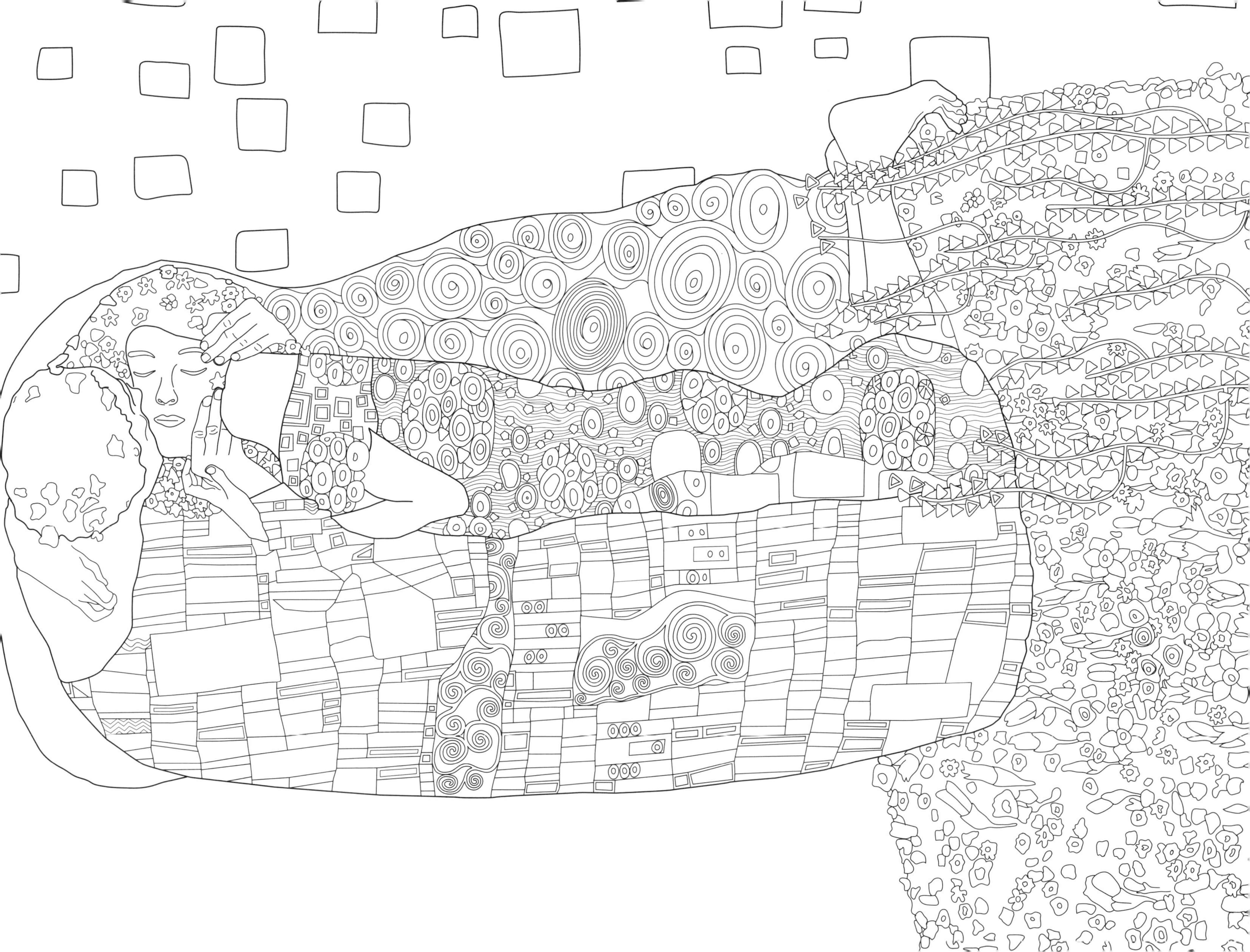

Nude Descending a Staircase, No. 2 1912

Marcel Duchamp 1887–1968

A lifelong innovator, French painter Marcel Duchamp blazed the trail that led to Pop art and Op art, and this is the work that not only established his reputation but also exhausted him. Intended for the Paris Salon des Indépendants exhibition of 1912, it appears to have been too 'independent' for the committee and was not accepted. Duchamp looked elsewhere and the painting travelled abroad, where it was seen at an exhibition in Barcelona before being moved on to New York City's Armory Show in 1913. The artist produced very little work thereafter.

The title may or may not refer to the image on the canvas, and critics have argued this point for more than a century. Certainly, there is not a great deal in the predominantly conical shapes that suggests human form. Instead, the focus is on the way Duchamp has suggested sweeping movement from the top left to the bottom right of the canvas. This effect is highlighted by the dark outline that simultaneously marks the edges of the figures and suggests rapid motion. The sense of movement is consolidated by the juxtaposition of the colours – a range of browns and ochres – and by the shades, which are lightest at the centre of the canvas and darken towards its edges, thereby reinforcing the impression that the centrepiece of the work is moving quickly.

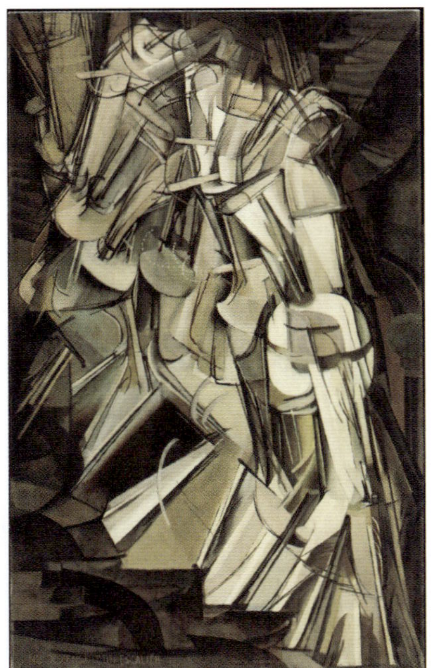

oil on canvas
147 cm × 89.2 cm
(57⅞ in. × 35⅛ in.)
Museum of Art, Philadelphia

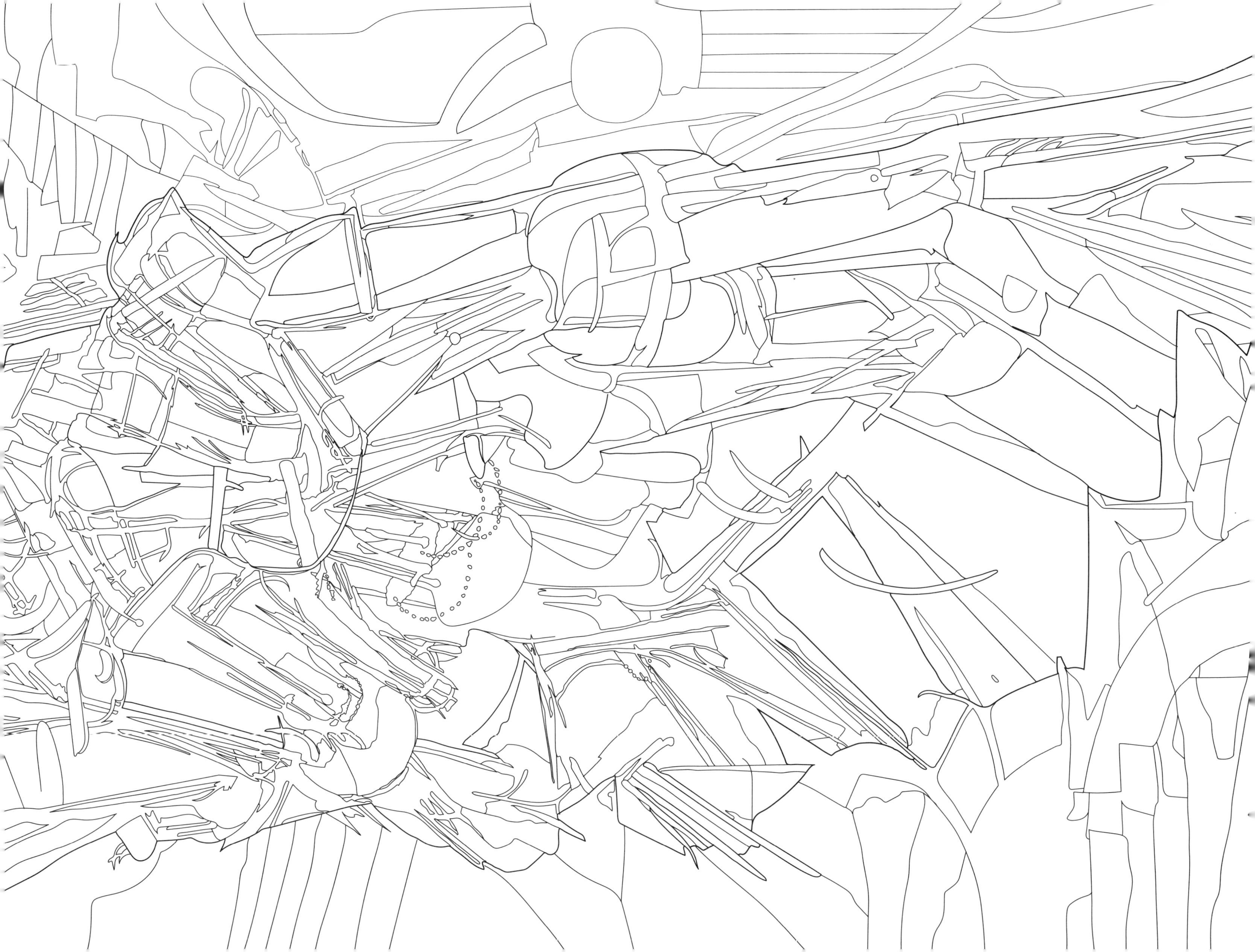

Still Life with a Guitar 1913

Juan Gris 1887 – 1927

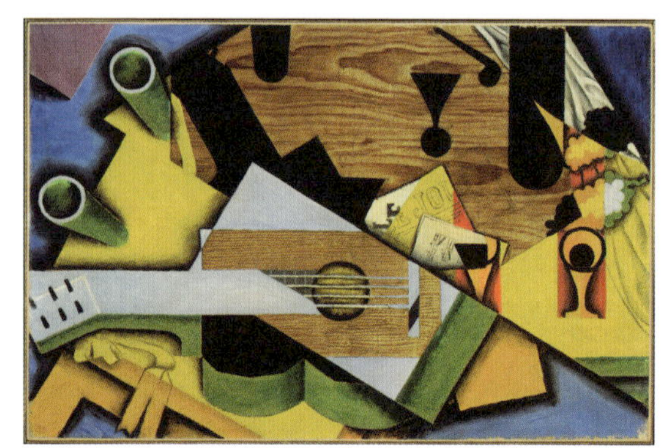

oil on canvas
66 cm × 100.3 cm
(26 in. × 39½ in.)
Metropolitan Museum of Art, New York

José Victoriano González studied engineering in his native Madrid and initially contributed drawings to illustrated newspapers. In his late teens he moved to Paris, where he took up residence with several artists and writers, adopted the name Juan Gris and began to paint seriously.

His talents were recognized and he achieved success relatively quickly, partly with the assistance of four contemporaries who were similarly destined for greatness. Gris was friends with Fernand Léger and Henri Matisse, but his two greatest influences were fellow Spaniard Pablo Picasso and Georges Braque. Gris adopted the Cubism of the latter pair and developed the style significantly: his preoccupation with mathematics in painting gave his artistic impulses an intellectual foundation. It was Gris who coined the term 'Analytical Cubism'.

Every element in this painting is portrayed with a classical precision of line, tone and pattern that makes a tightly interlocked whole, without any unnecessary embellishment. This is a deliberate attempt to make the viewer see perspective in a new way: the scene may seem basic and flat at first glance, but the longer we look, the more three-dimensional it appears to be, starting with the two green cylinders on the left of the canvas and extending to the green sides of the guitar. In addition to the order and geometry seen here, Gris also favoured daring combinations of bright colours.

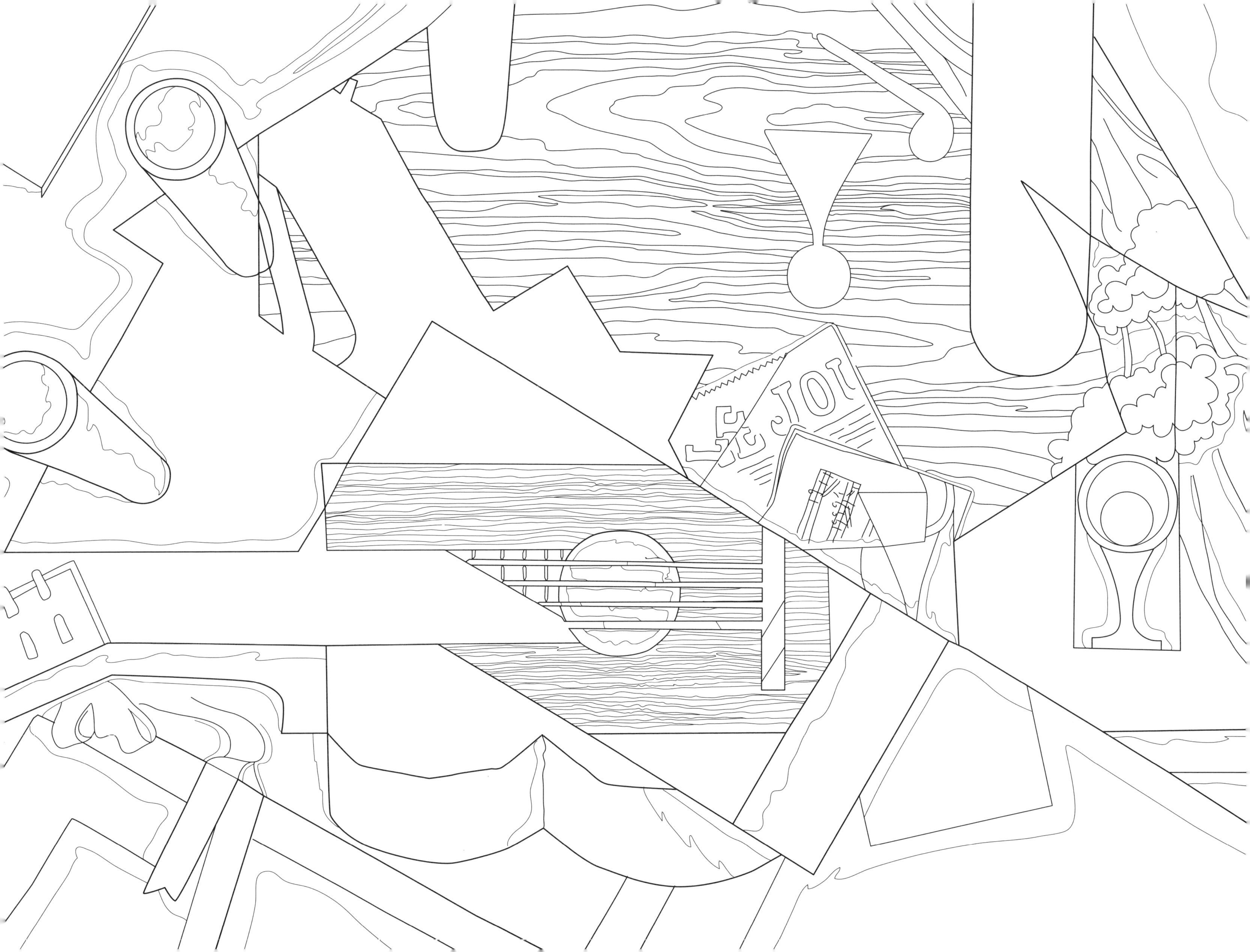

LE JOU

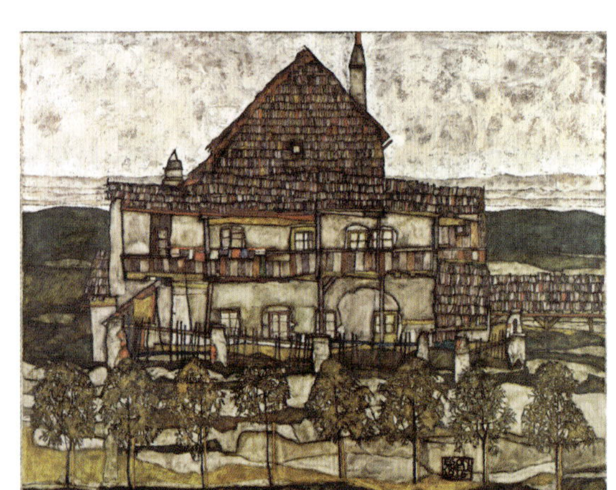

oil on canvas
110 cm × 140 cm
(43⅜ in. × 55⅛ in.)
Leopold Museum, Vienna

House with Shingles 1915

Egon Schiele 1890 – 1918

Egon Schiele was an Austrian artist who had two main early influences: the Jugendstil movement (the German Art Nouveau) and Gustav Klimt, leader of the Vienna Secession group, whom he knew personally. Schiele created numerous nude portraits, many based on models so young that he outraged public opinion, and an extensive series of urban landscapes, which are distinguished by their outstanding draughtsmanship and decorative elegance. He achieved great things and was on the brink of further success when he died at the age of twenty-eight, one of twenty million victims of the Spanish flu epidemic that swept Europe at the end of World War I.

The house depicted here has a dynamic quality that is derived from the setting: within the landscape, but oddly apart from it. This effect is achieved by the arrangement of the trees, wall, fields and background hills. The positioning of these in strongly parallel lines makes the building look as if it is passing through the scene, like a ship. Every building block is surrounded by a strong black outline, which emphasizes the overlapping arrangement of the shingle.

At first glance, the predominant tone throughout the canvas appears to be yellowish brown, but note how subtly the base colour blends into the trees at the foot of the canvas and the red on the balcony. It even makes its presence visible in the green expanse across the middle.

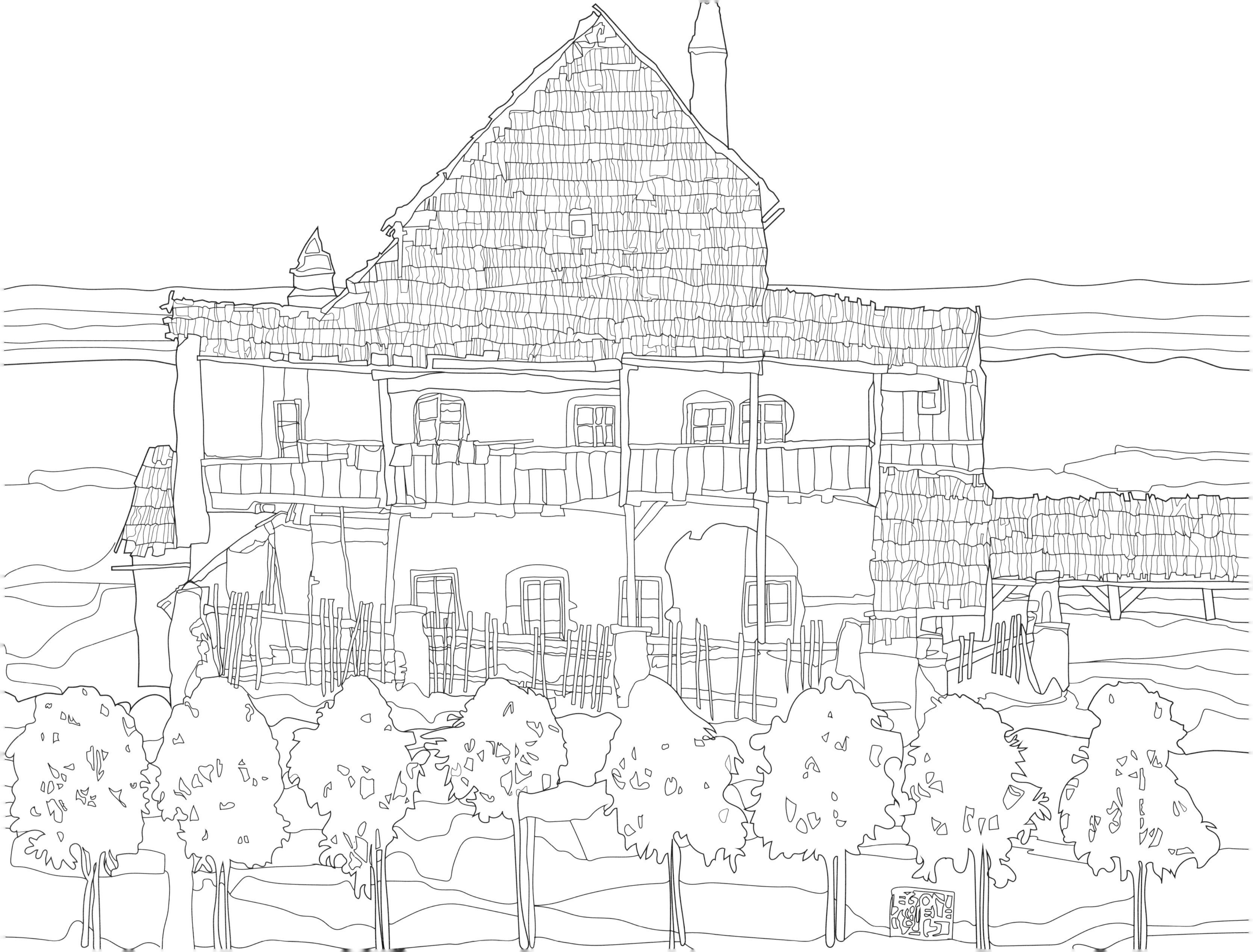

Portrait of Madame Kisling c. 1917
Amadeo Modigliani 1884 – 1920

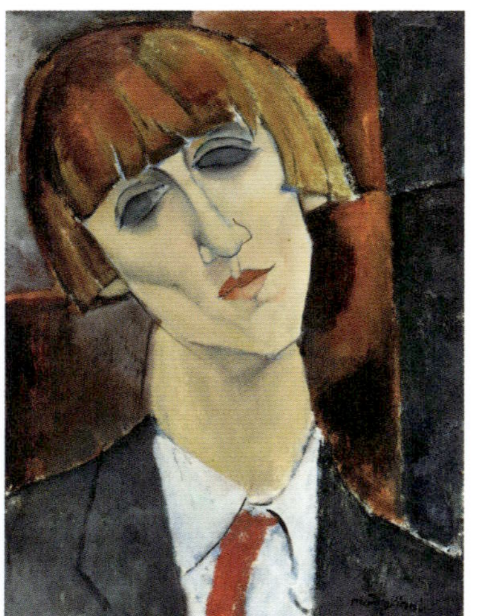

oil on canvas
46.2 cm x 33.2 cm
(18¼ in. x 13⅛ in.)
National Gallery of Art, Washington DC

Amadeo Modigliani was born in Livorno, Italy, and suffered from poor health as a child, which meant that he was unable to receive a formal education. He spent most of his short and unhappy life in Paris, where he painted and sculpted with little financial or critical success, and rarely participated in exhibitions. In 1917 he had a solo show organized at a gallery, but what might have been a breakthrough ended in humiliation – his paintings of female nudes outraged public decency, and the exhibition was closed by French police on the opening day. The artist received global acclaim only after his death from tubercular meningitis at the age of thirty-five.

Modigliani painted several formal portraits of contemporary artists residing in Paris, including Pablo Picasso, Diego Rivera, Juan Gris and Moïse Kisling. This work depicts Kisling's wife Renée, a renowned society hostess and photographer whose images are some of the most striking evocations of *les années folles* (the mad years), which marked the Roaring Twenties in the French capital. Madame Kisling's sharp features lent themselves well to Modigliani's clean lines and angular style: her features are almost sculptural. The tilted angle of her head and the eyes directed downwards suggest a meditative and reflective personality. Her vivid auburn hair is counterbalanced by the red necktie, which was regarded at the time as very avant-garde clothing for a woman.

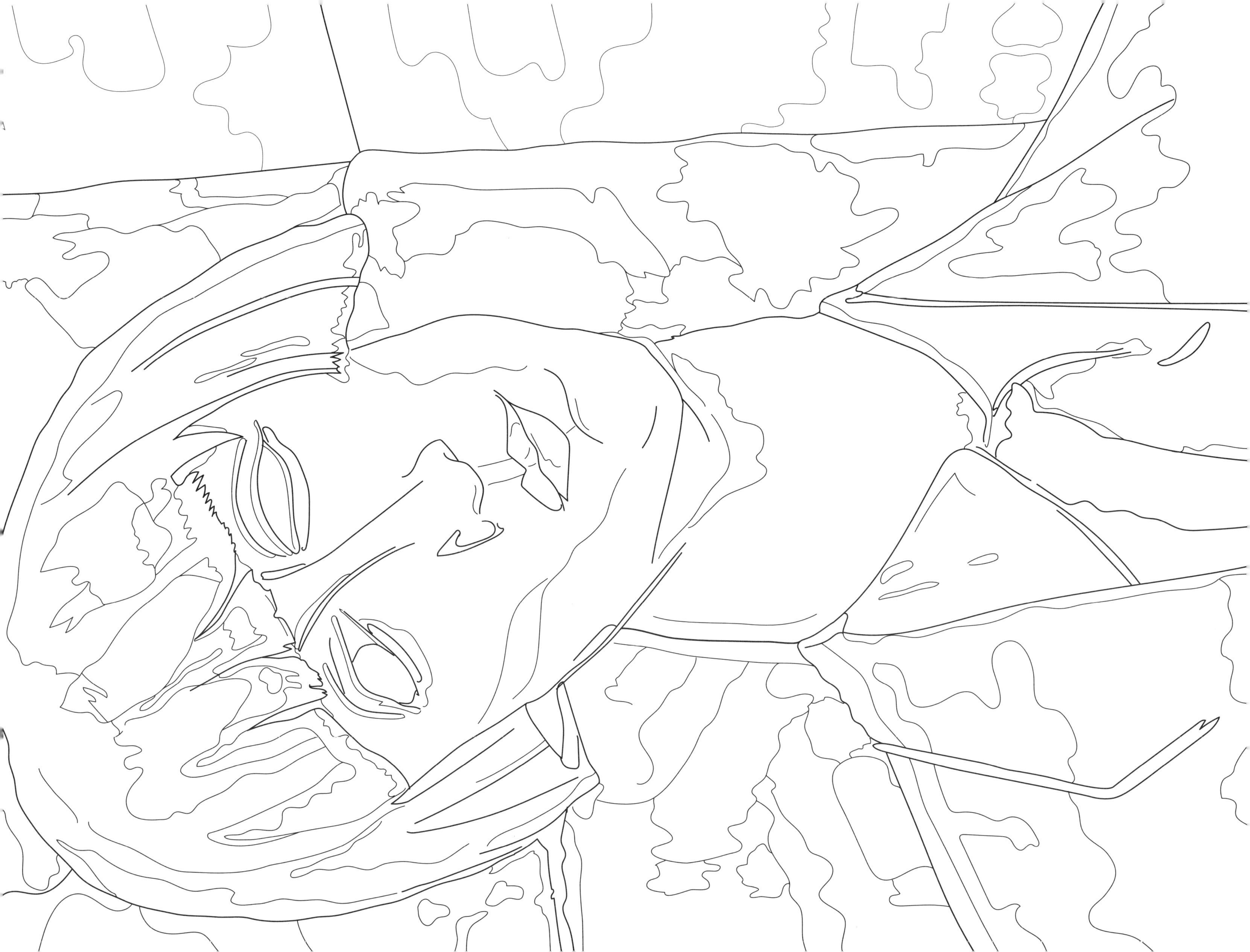

Bird Garden 1924

Paul Klee 1879–1940

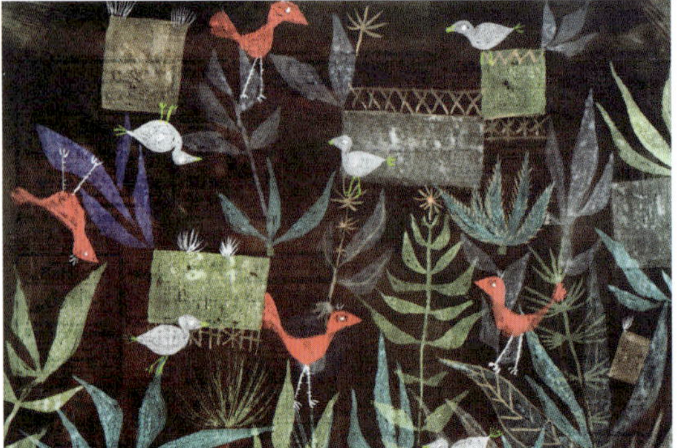

watercolour and oil transfer drawing on newspaper
27 cm × 39 cm
(10 $\frac{5}{8}$ in. × 15 $\frac{3}{8}$ in.)
Pinakothek der Moderne, Munich

Although Paul Klee was born in Switzerland and had a Swiss mother, under Swiss law every child had to take the nationality of his or her father, who in Klee's case was German. This enabled him to finance his painting by teaching at the Bauhaus schools in Weimar, Dusseldorf and Berlin, but when the Nazi Party came to power in 1933 it denounced Klee's work as degenerate. Consequently, he returned to his native land where he spent the rest of his life.

The artist's paintings are often described as having a musical quality. Certainly, he was a talented violinist who might in other circumstances have turned professional, but it seems more likely that the term is used because his work does not conform to any of the conventional groupings of his period: it shows the influence of Expressionism, Cubism and Surrealism, but does not sit comfortably within any of these movements.

One of the most striking qualities of *Bird Garden* is its playful exploration of weightlessness: the red and grey birds walk across the murky, earthy greens of the grass and foliage, but make no impression on them. This is probably a dream, but unlike so many dreams in art, there is no hidden threat: none of the birds is in the air, because they have no need to be. If it is not a reverie, perhaps it is paradise. Close examination of the original work reveals some of the newsprint on which it was painted.

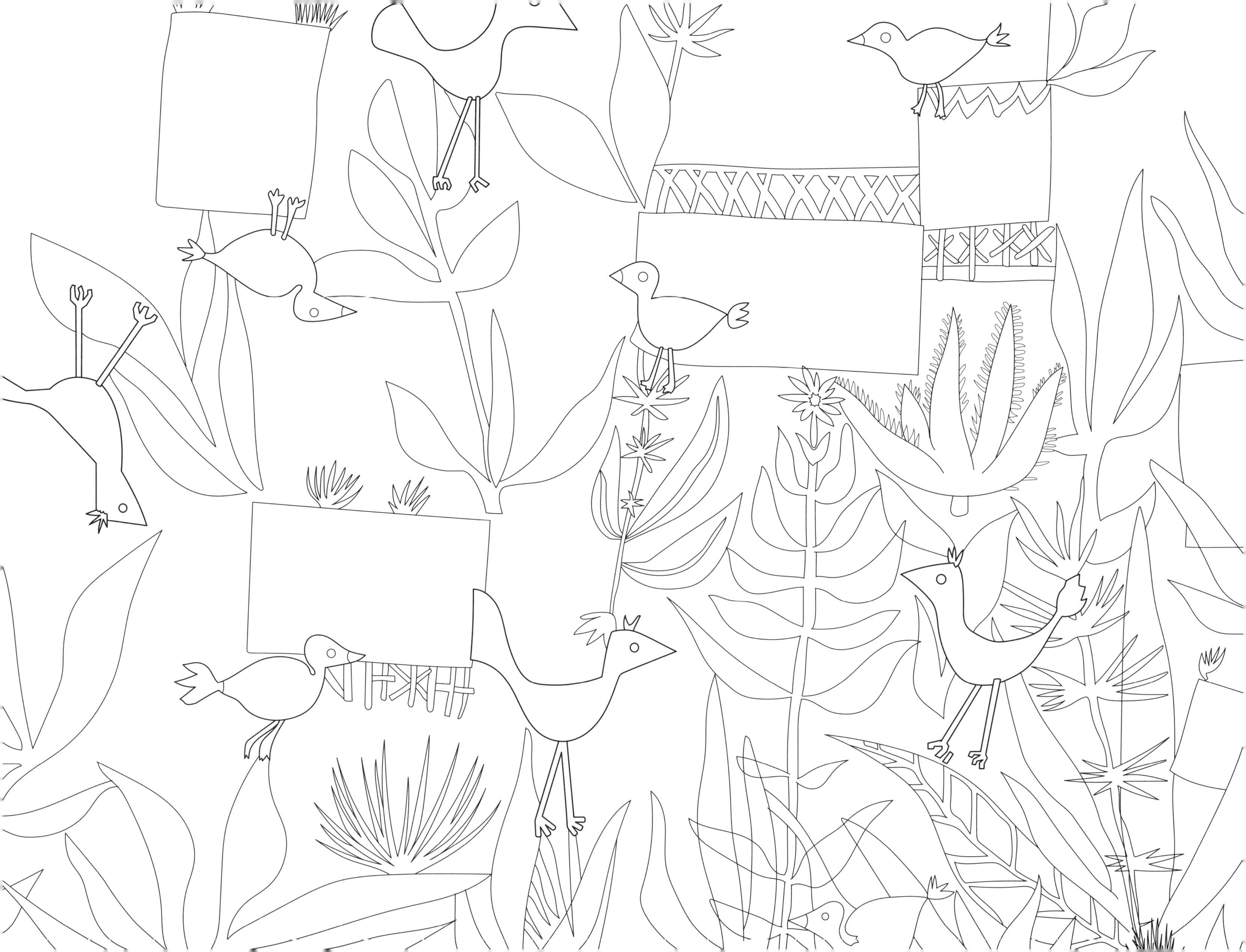

Carnival of Harlequin 1924 – 25

Joan Miró 1893 – 1983

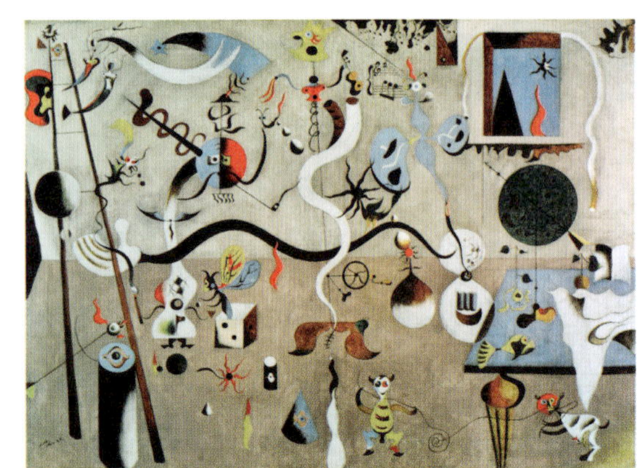

oil on canvas
66 cm × 90.5 cm
(26 in. × 35 ⅝ in.)
Albright–Knox Art Gallery, Buffalo

Although Joan Miró was born in Barcelona and lived most of his life there or in Mallorca, he painted this canvas in Paris, where he spent time periodically with the poet André Breton and other Surrealists. Miró was never strongly associated with this group, and did not subscribe fully to some of its more extreme hypotheses about the relation of the subconscious to waking thoughts and actions. However, Surrealism gave him the freedom to indulge his expansive pictorial fantasies, which could then be intellectualized as variations on Freudian themes. In truth, Miró derived his greatest pleasures from shapes and colours, rather than from high-brow theories about their psychological significance.

   Carnival of Harlequin is a riot of multicoloured geometric shapes. The title character is the sad-looking guitar figure on the left of the canvas, recognizable by his black-and-white shirt, moustache, pipe and headgear. The central sinuous lines – the vertical one white, the horizontal one black – are open to interpretation, but there is no doubt about several of the other figures: two cats play with a ball of wool in the bottom right corner and a dragonfly emerges like a jack-in-the-box from a playing die by the harlequin. Through the window in the top right corner, we can see a black triangle, which represents the Eiffel Tower, and two other indeterminate objects, perhaps a tree and a star.

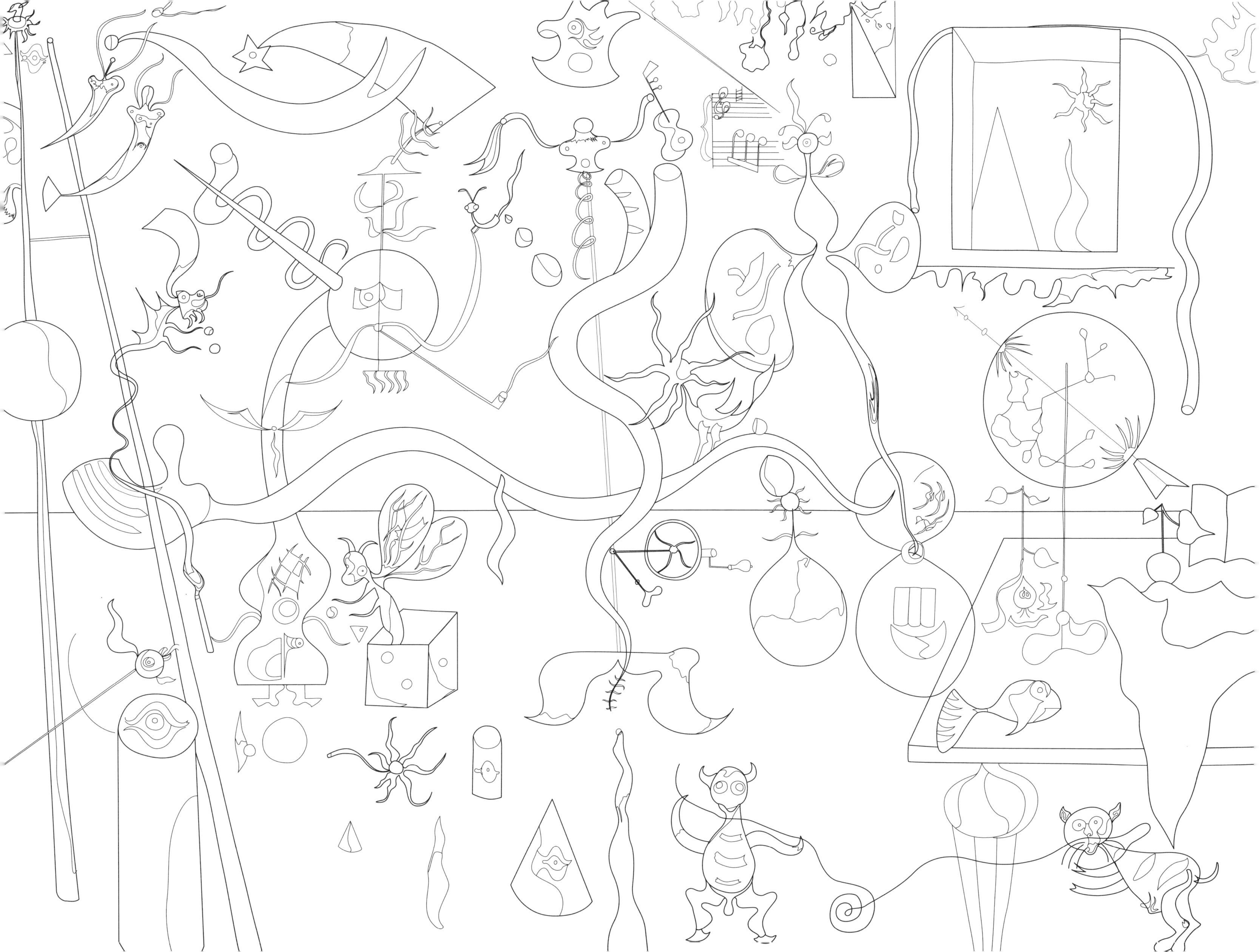

Yellow, Red, Blue 1925

Wassily Kandinsky 1866–1944

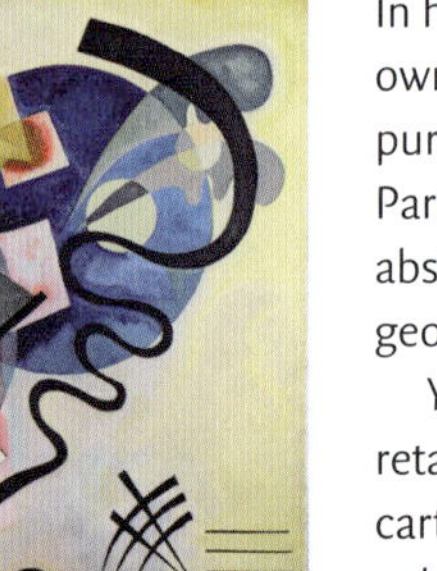

oil on canvas
128 cm × 201.5 cm
(50 ⅜ in. × 79 ⅜ in.)
Musée National d'Art Moderne, Paris

In his youth, Wassily Kandinsky believed that every colour had a life of its own. He originally trained as a lawyer before leaving his native Moscow to pursue his dream of becoming an artist, dividing his time between Munich, Paris and Berlin. Having helped to found German Expressionism and then abstract art, in the 1920s he began to concentrate increasingly on pure geometric forms.

Yellow, Red, Blue is a work that embodies this change of direction. It retains a level of ambiguity, but the abstract elements are bounded by cartoon-like chequerboards, squares, circles and triangles in bold primary colours. Black lines – some straight, others curved – intersect the colours and shapes; these are thickest and most prominent on the right of the canvas, whereas the left side of the painting has finer lines and paler colours. Kandinsky intended these contrasts to make the viewer think about the ways in which the two halves of the painting interact: to what extent are they complementary, and to what extent are they in opposition?

There is no correct answer to these questions, but the artist certainly hoped to fire viewers' imaginations with this work. Indeed, many people have claimed to see faces and creatures hidden within the composition, especially when it is looked at upside down. Kandinsky may not have placed these figures there intentionally, but he did mean to inspire fantasies.

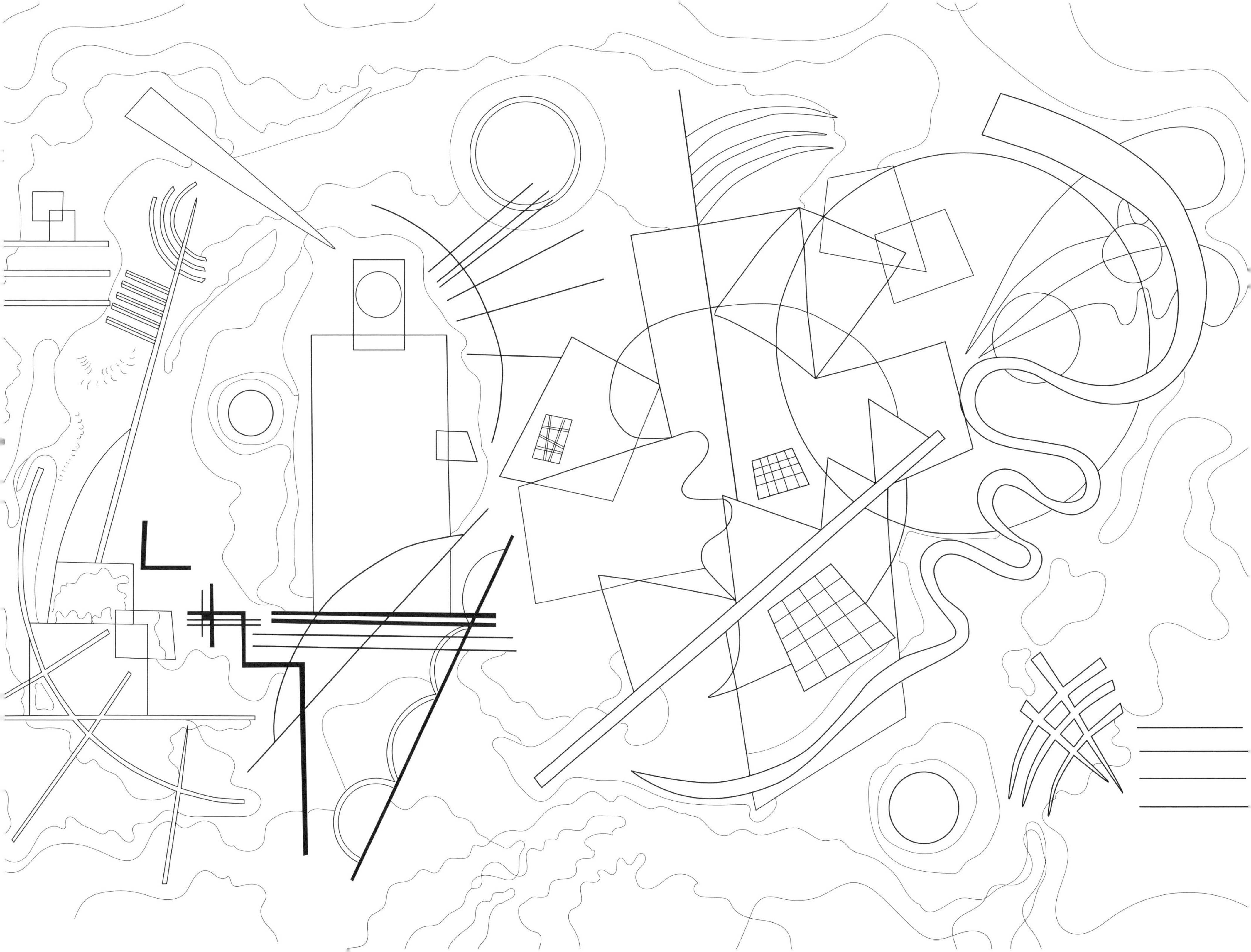

Swans Reflecting Elephants 1937
Salvador Dalí 1904 – 1989

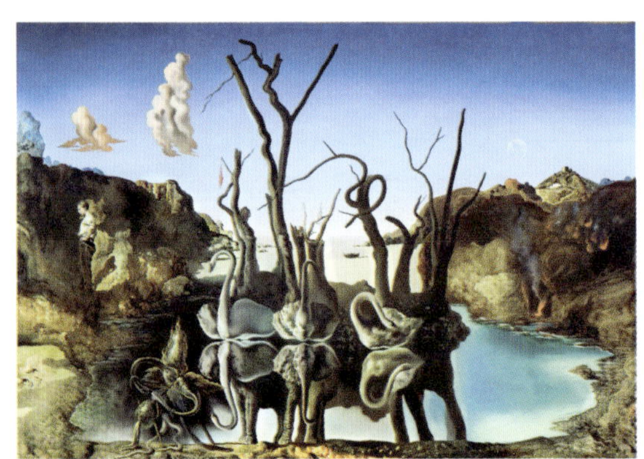

oil on canvas
51 cm × 77 cm
(20 in. × 30⅜ in.)
Private collection

Salvador Dalí hailed from the Catalonia region of Spain and revealed precocious talent as an art student in Madrid and Barcelona, despite not developing a mature style of his own until he was in his late twenties. By this time, he had immersed himself in Sigmund Freud's writings on suppressed sexual urges and had associated himself with the Paris Surrealists, who sought in their art to reflect their ultimate truth: that the subconscious was a higher power than reason. Thereafter, Dalí endeavoured to bring to the surface some of the images buried in his own subconscious, and capture them for posterity.

His method may seem odd, but the results are undoubtedly spectacular. In this painting, and in many other works, Dalí depicts the way that, in dreams, one vision may bleed into another for no easily identifiable reason. Here, the artist uses the reflective surface of the lake to create a double image: the three swans are reflected in the lake so that their necks become the elephants' trunks and the trees become the elephants' legs. The swans are not painted in a fully white swan-like colour and the elephants are not a fully grey elephant-like colour: the creatures merge into each other.

In the background, the landscape is full of the fiery reds and browns seen in Catalonia in the autumn. The cliffs are rendered with swirling brushwork to emphasize the stillness of the lake.

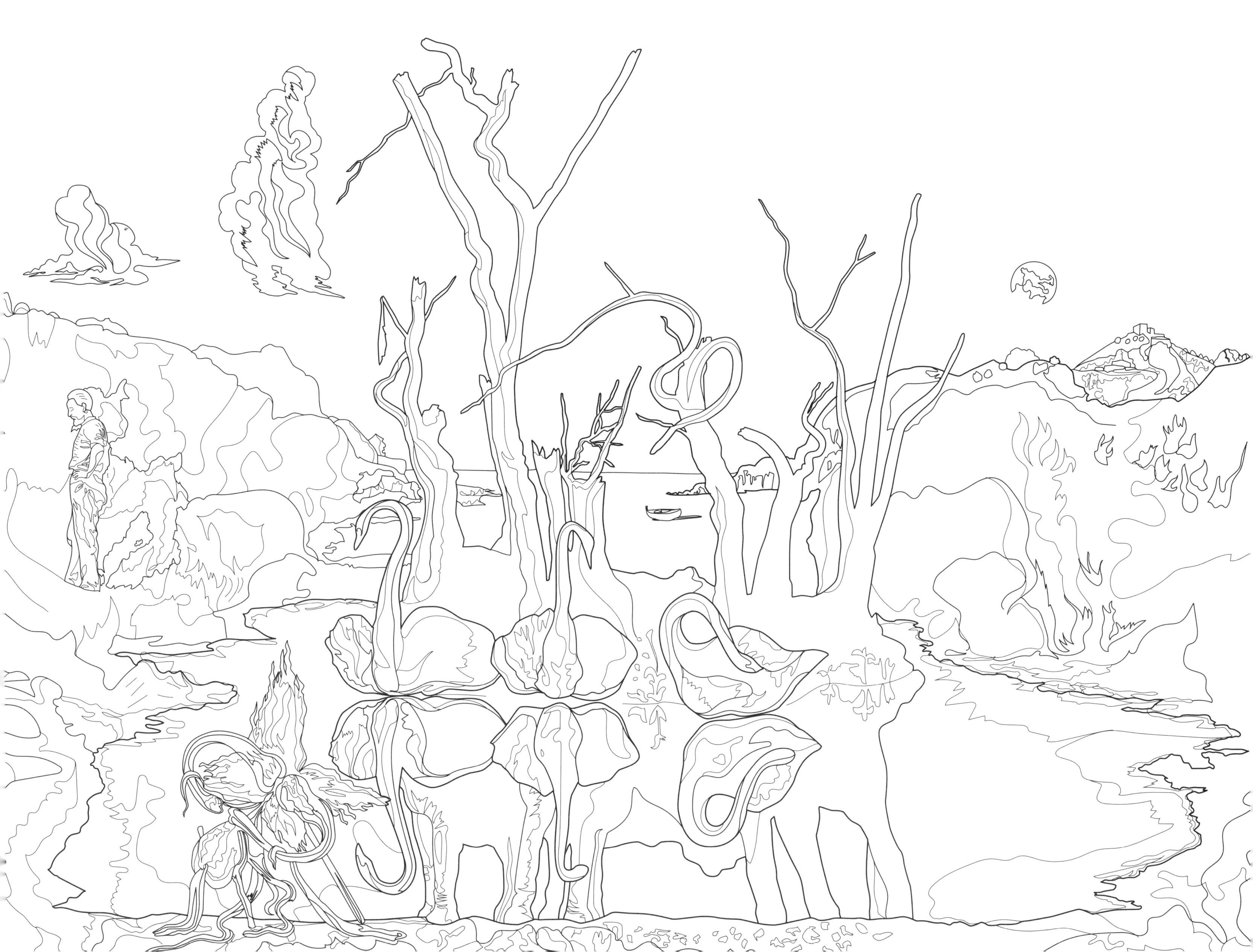

Self-portrait with Thorn Necklace and Hummingbird 1940

Frida Kahlo 1907 – 1954

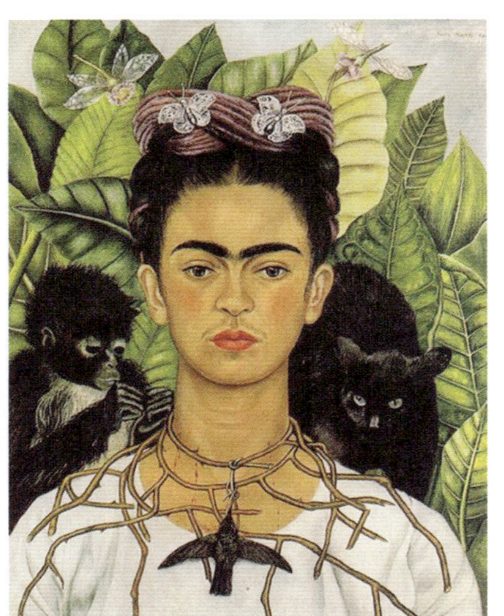

oil on canvas
61.25 cm × 47 cm
(24⅛ in. × 18½ in.)
University of Texas at Austin

The life of Frida Kahlo was full of pain, both physical and emotional. She was a childhood victim of polio, and at the age of eighteen she was hit by a bus and never fully recovered from her injuries. She painted this self-portrait in the same year in which she divorced her husband, Diego Rivera, another great Mexican artist, and broke up with her long-time lover, Hungarian-American photographer Nickolas Muray.

The work is brimming with highly ambivalent symbolism. The expression 'a monkey on my back', meaning a burden that you cannot shake loose, has been taken to represent Rivera. Although the hummingbird may signify good luck in Western culture, in the pre-Columbian Aztec civilization of Mexico it was an avatar of the god of war; in either case, here the creature is dead. The black cat, too, is an uncertain presence: it could be a good or a bad omen, but it seems to have its eyes on the bird.

What is perfectly straightforward, however, is the blood on Kahlo's neck that has been drawn by the thorns sticking into her skin. There is not a great deal of red on the canvas, but it dominates the green of the foliage, the black of the animals' fur and Kahlo's hair, and the white of her dress. Note also the shadows below her eyes and the trace of a moustache above the line of her top lip. Undoubtedly, the artist wants the viewer to recognize her suffering.

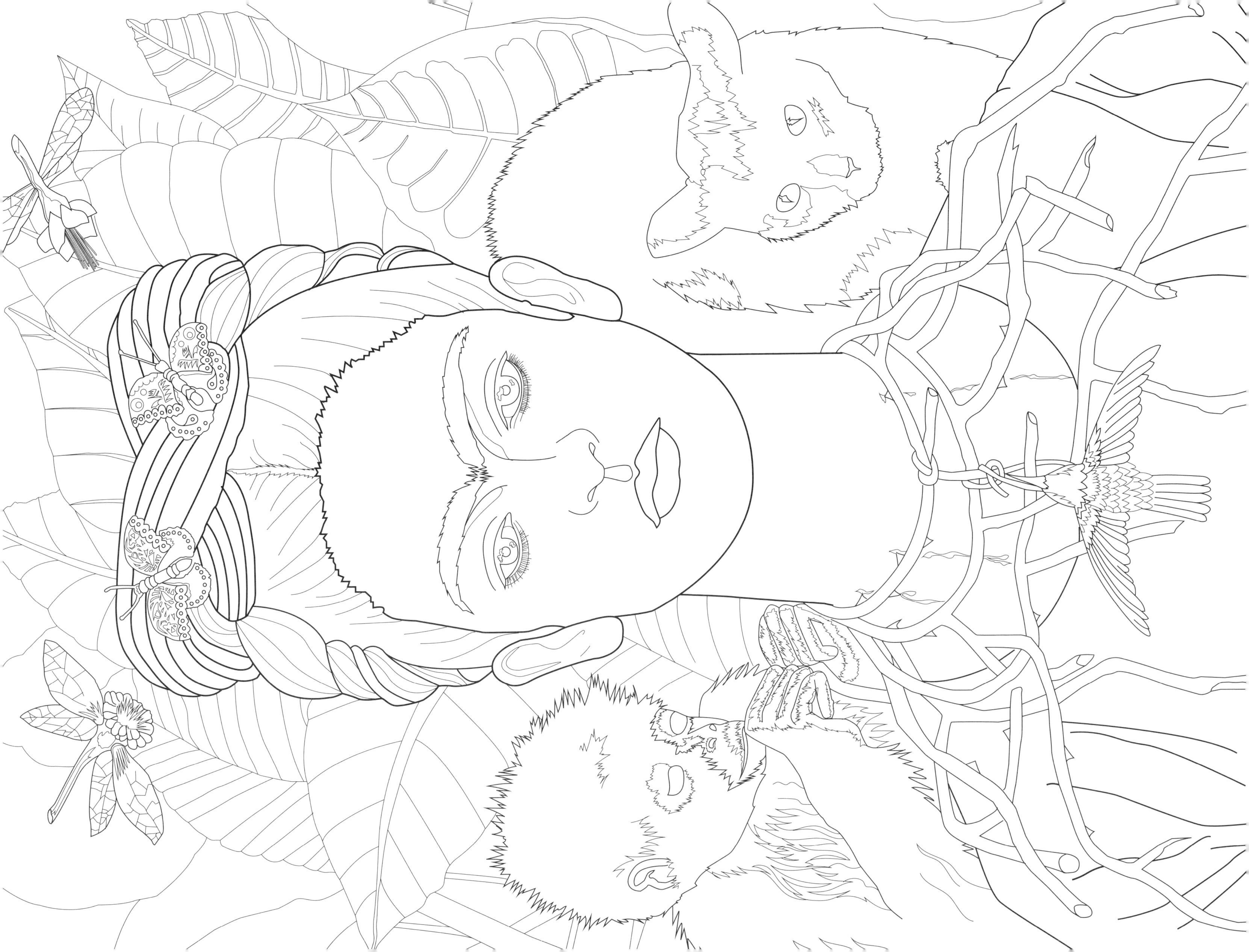

Whaam! 1963

Roy Lichtenstein 1923–1997

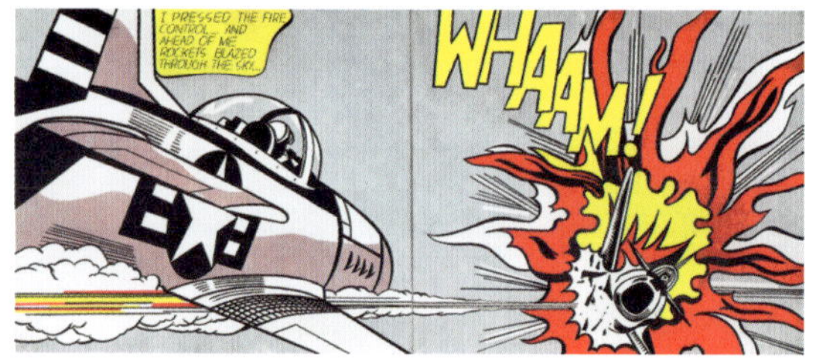

acrylic and oil on canvas
172.7 cm × 406.4 cm
(68 in. × 13 ft 4 in.)
Tate Modern, London

New Yorker Roy Lichtenstein was one of the founders of Pop art, which incorporated painting styles that had previously been regarded as too lowbrow to be worthy of critical acclaim. In his youth, Lichtenstein experimented with various classical forms and with Abstract Expressionism, but he soon developed a preference for the comic strip. It was not that he was a fan of comics as such – he had been brought up to take the conventional view in the 1930s that they were not worth looking at – but he wanted to challenge himself to bring art into an unconventional setting, and one that was regarded as art's antithesis. The use of text in the composition might at first seem unusual but it was not a new idea. It appears in works from ancient Egypt and medieval times, as well as more recently in Cubism.

One of Lichtenstein's most important works, *Whaam!* is a diptych. It is painted on two canvases – the warplane on one panel, and its target on the other – which are linked stylistically by the streak of gunfire (opposite) travelling between the two aircraft. It is adapted from a panel by Irv Novick from the 'Star Jockey' story in issue 89 of *All-American Men of War* published by DC Comics in February 1962. Across the background and on areas of the attacking warplane, Lichtenstein has used stencilled dots, known as Benday dots after printer and illustrator Benjamin Day. These may prove a considerable challenge for the colourist to reproduce.

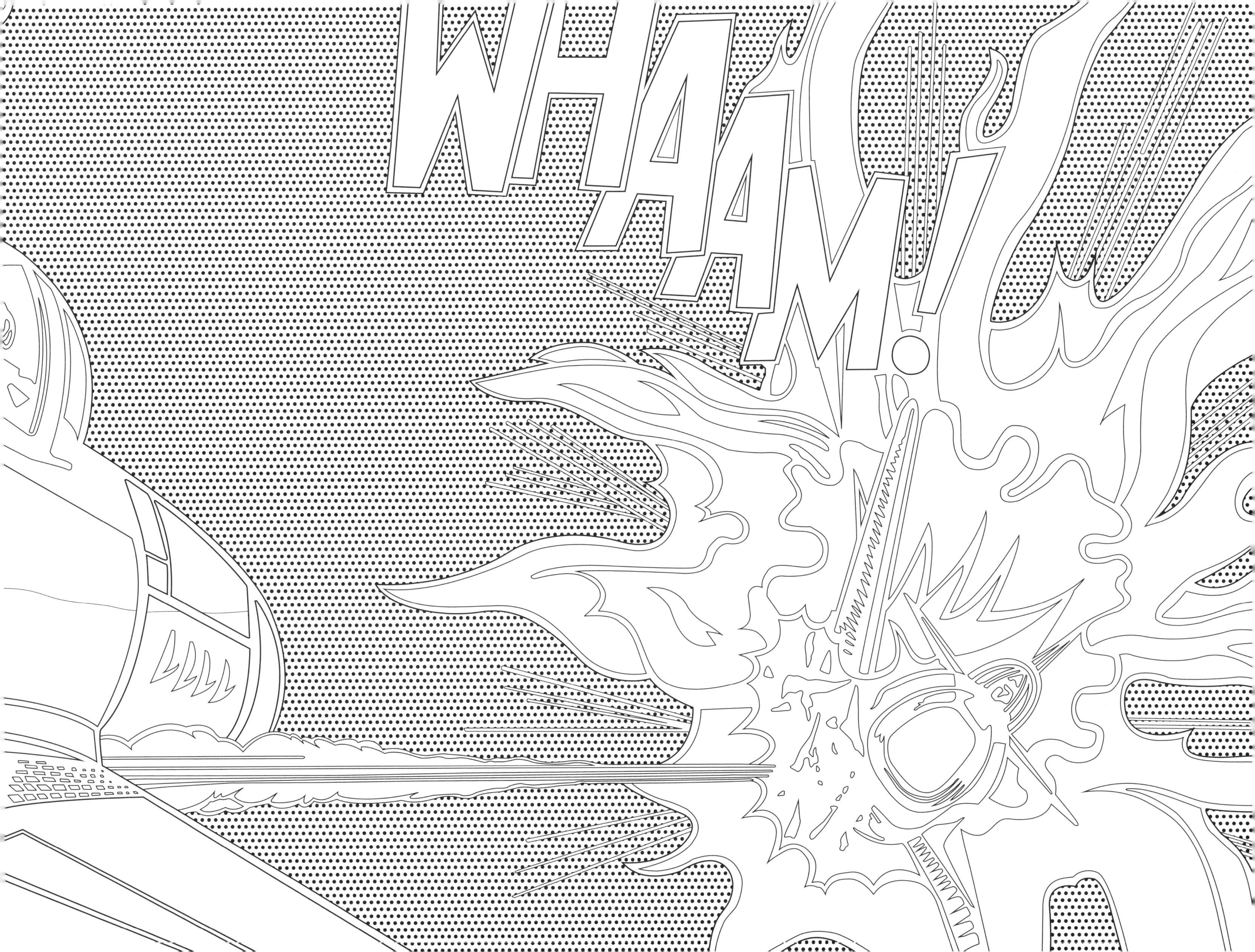

WHAAM!

Untitled (Dancing Dogs) 1981

Keith Haring 1958 – 1990

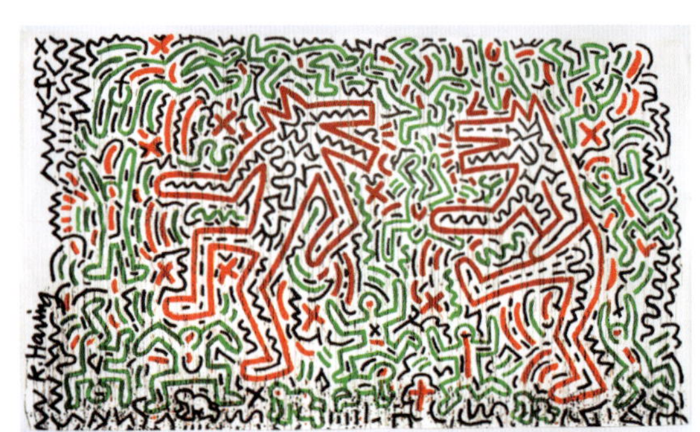

sumi ink and acrylic on paper mounted on canvas
274.3 cm × 486.4 cm
(9 ft × 16 ft)
Private collection

Keith Haring began to create public drawings in chalk on blank black advertising panels in New York City's subways in 1980. Thanks to his easily recognizable style, readily understandable symbolism and strong sense of fun, his urban art was soon in big demand across the United States and in many other countries around the world. Much of his work was committed to social change and was particularly concerned with drug control and the awareness of AIDS, the disease from which he died at the age of thirty-one.

Haring is well known for his frieze-like compositions, described by the Museum of Modern Art in New York as 'resolutely horizontal'. This work may seem difficult to decipher at first glance, especially in one of its many black and white reproductions, but gradually the intricate patterning comes together in more recognizable forms. First into view are the two canines from the unofficial title. Later, the viewer notices the human figures, many of which appear to be falling and closely resemble the chalk lines drawn around corpses at crime scenes.

In Haring's original drawing, the dancing dogs are red in outline and the other figures bounded by green, but colourists can have fun picking out and filling in each individual depiction in complementary or contrasting shades of their own choice.

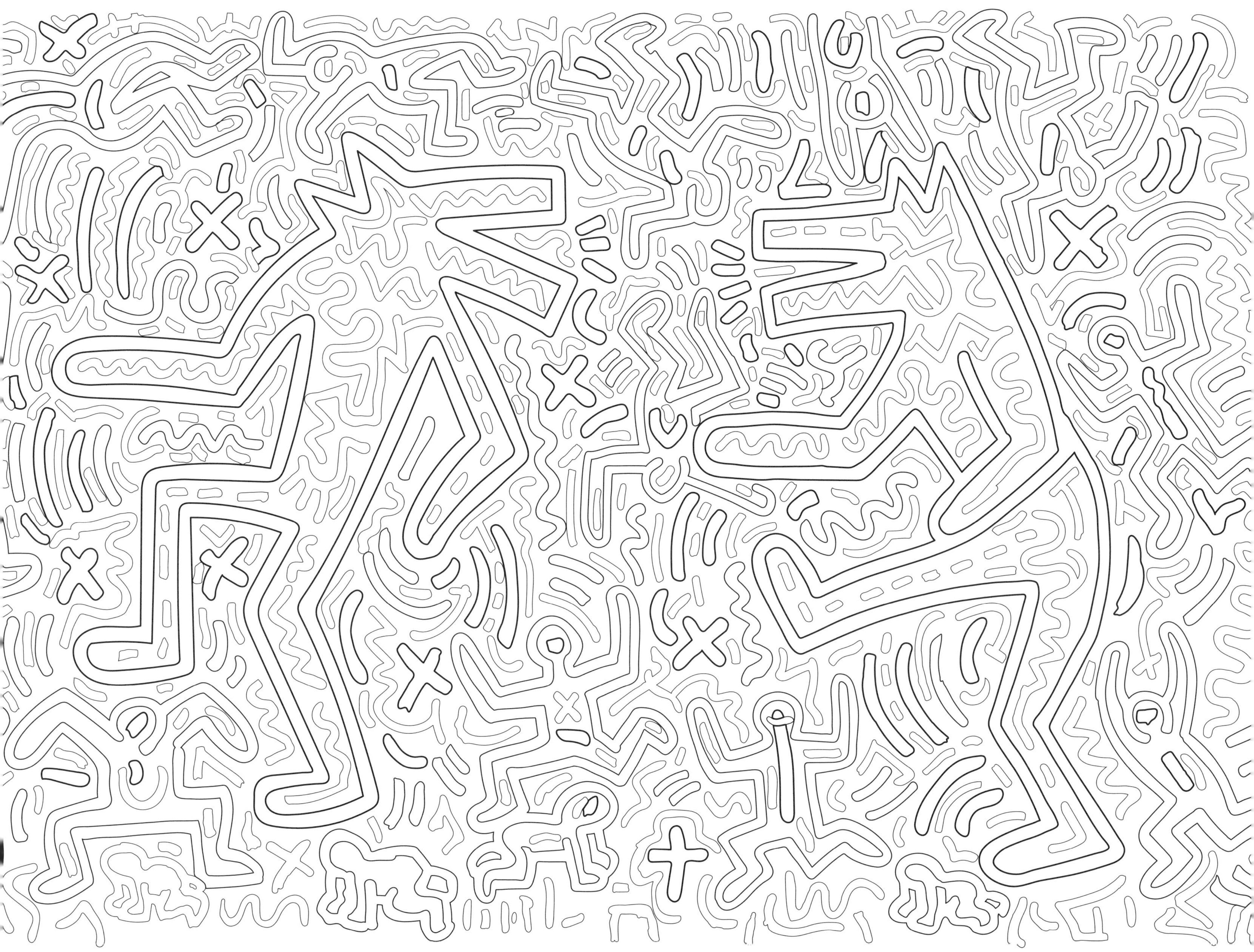

Carpet Snake and Kangaroo Dreaming at Mt Denison 1993

Clifford Possum Tjapaltjarri c. 1932 – 2002

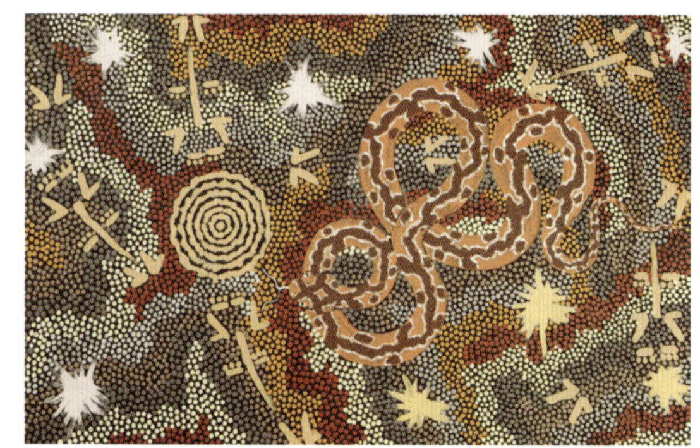

acrylic on linen
60 cm × 85 cm
(23 ⅝ in. × 33 ½ in.)
Private collection

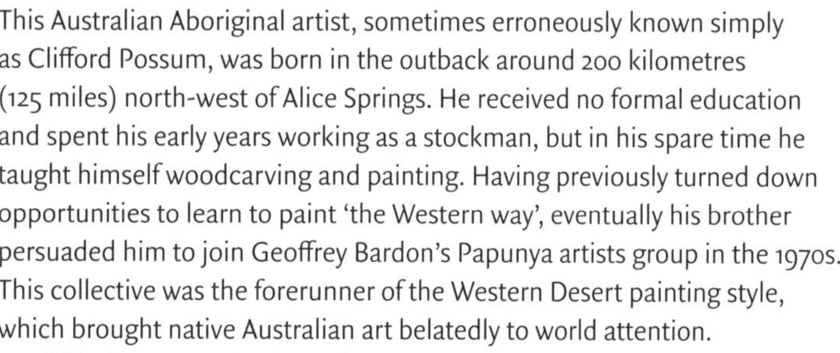

This Australian Aboriginal artist, sometimes erroneously known simply as Clifford Possum, was born in the outback around 200 kilometres (125 miles) north-west of Alice Springs. He received no formal education and spent his early years working as a stockman, but in his spare time he taught himself woodcarving and painting. Having previously turned down opportunities to learn to paint 'the Western way', eventually his brother persuaded him to join Geoffrey Bardon's Papunya artists group in the 1970s. This collective was the forerunner of the Western Desert painting style, which brought native Australian art belatedly to world attention.

Clifford Possum Tjapaltjarri became the most important member of the movement. In the latter stages of his career, his work incorporated increasingly complex and diverse iconography, but his reputation was built initially on dot art, such as the work shown here. Mount Denison lies in the south of the Northern Territory, only 850 metres (2,800 ft) above sea level. 'Dreaming' refers to Aboriginal creation myths, in this case an encounter between a snake and a kangaroo. The main colours are browns and yellows, but there is also plenty of green. This last seems to seep into the texture in much the same way as the progress of the legendary snake across the desert carved out valleys that became watercourses, and the bouncing of the kangaroo created uplands and lowlands.

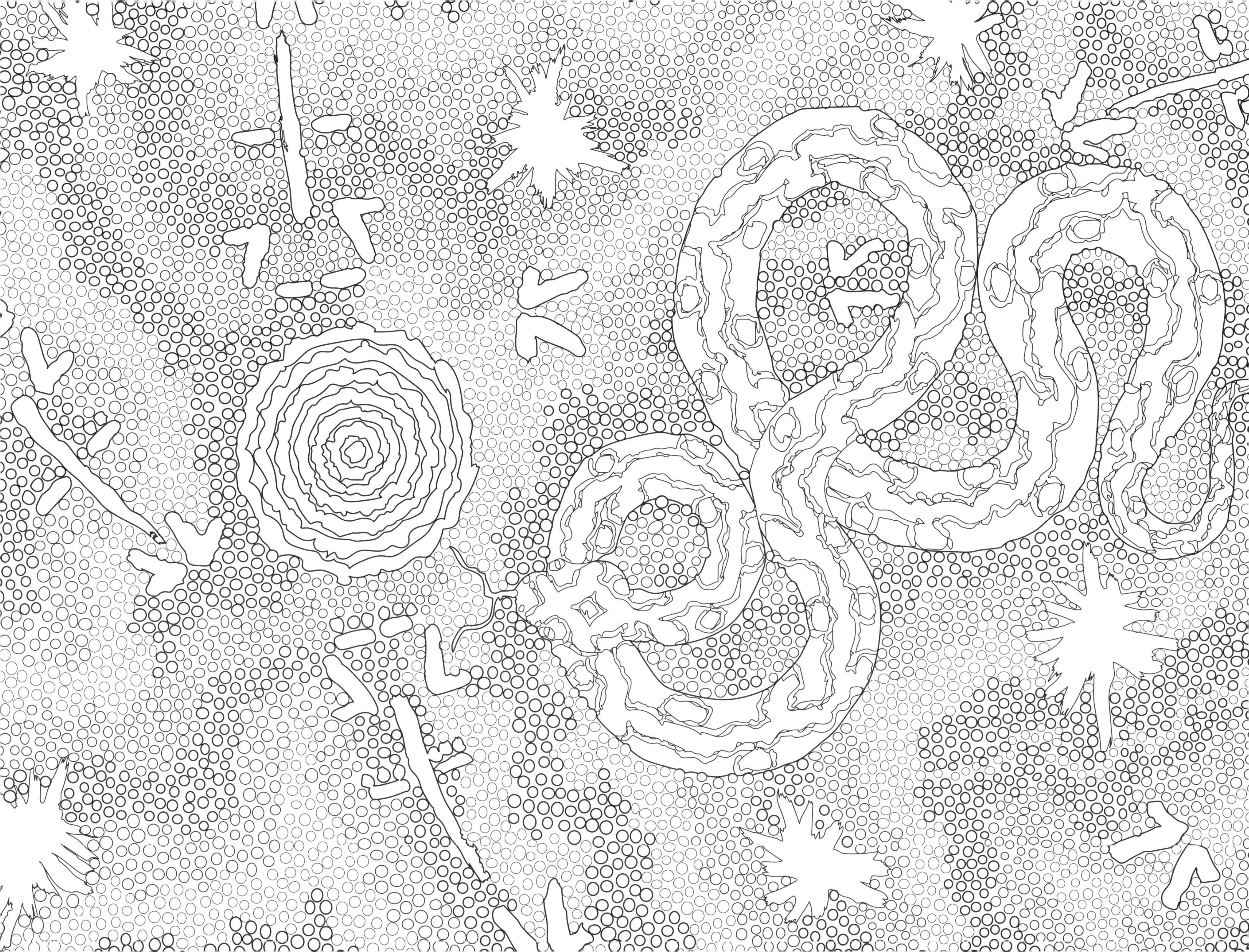

First published in the United Kingdom in 2016 by
Thames & Hudson Ltd, 6-24 Britannia Street,
London WC1X 9JD

Reprinted 2023, 2024, 2026

This book was designed and produced by Quintessence,
an imprint of The Quarto Group
1 Triptych Place
London SE1 9SH

Project Editor   Hannah Phillips
Designers   Isabel Eeles, Josse Pickard
Editorial Director   Ruth Patrick
Publisher   Philip Cooper

EU Authorized Representative Interart S.A.R.L.
19 rue Charles Auray, 93500 Pantin, Paris, France
productsafety@thameshudson.co.uk
www.interart.fr

A CIP catalogue record for this book is available from the British Library

ISBN 978-0-500-29268-6
04

Printed in China

All works are courtesy of the museums, galleries or collections listed in the
individual captions.

10 Wikimedia Commons: Codex Nuttall p.16, User: HJPD, URL: https://commons.wikimedia.
org/wiki/File:CNuttall16.jpg, https://creativecommons.org/licenses/by/3.0/deed.en
16 Galleria degli Uffizi, Florence, Italy / Bridgeman Images **18** Heritage Image
Partnership Ltd / Alamy Stock Photo **42** The Museum of Fine Arts, Houston, The
Robert Lee Blaffer Memorial Collection, gift of Sarah Cambell Blaffer **50** Buyenlarge/
Getty Images **58** Artepics / Alamy Stock Photo **68** PAINTING / Alamy Stock Photo
72 Heritage Image Partnership Ltd / Alamy Stock Photo / © Succession Marcel
Duchamp / ADAGP, Paris and DACS, London 2016 **76** Fine Art Images / Heritage
Images / Getty Images **80** Bayerische Staatsgemaldesammlungen / Bridgeman Images
82 The Art Archive / Albright-Knox Art Gallery Buffalo / Superstock / © Successió
Miró / ADAGP, Paris and DACS London 2016 **84** Peter Willi / Bridgeman Images
86 Heritage Image Partnership Ltd / Alamy Stock Photo / © Salvador Dali, Fundació Gala-
Salvador Dalí, DACS 2016 **88** The Artchives / Alamy Stock Photo / © Banco de México
Diego Rivera Frida Kahlo Museums Trust, Mexico, D.F. / DACS 2016 **90** akg-images / Erich
Lessing / © Estate of Roy Lichtenstein / DACS 2016 **92** © The Keith Haring Foundation
94 © Aboriginal Art World Pty Ltd / © The Estate of Clifford Possum Tjapaltjarri licensed by
DACS / AAA / VISCOPY 2016